D0398529

*I hope this book
helps you live a life
you love — today and
every day.*

Beth Sawi

COMING
UP
FOR AIR

COMING
UP

How to
Build a
Balanced Life
in a
Workaholic World

FOR AIR

BETH SAWI

HYPERION   New York

Copyright © 2000 Beth Sawi

All rights reserved. No part of this book may be used or reproduced in any manner whatsoever without the written permission of the Publisher. Printed in the United States of America. For information address: Hyperion, 77 West 66th Street, New York, NY 10023-6298.

Library of Congress Cataloging-in-Publication Data

Sawi, Beth
    Coming up for air : how to build a balanced life in a workaholic world / by Beth Sawi.
        p.   cm.
    Includes bibliographic references.
    1. Work and family.   2. Quality of work life.   I. Title.
HD4904.25.S33   2000
640'.43—dc21   99-38227
                                                                                    CIP

ISBN 0-7868-6549-0

Design by Abby Kagan

FIRST EDITION

10   9   8   7   6   5   4   3   2

This book is dedicated to all the people
who told me the stories of their own trials and joys
in search for balance.
Your voices brought this book to life. Thank you.

Contents

Acknowledgments

My greatest thank-you goes to all the people who have let me peek into their lives and learn about the struggles they've had with finding balance. This particularly applies to those who have attended my Balanced Life courses and willingly participated in an environment where we all learned together.

I'd also like to thank my dear friend Nicole Young, who nudged me down the path to being a writer. Without her support and enthusiasm, I never would have attempted this book.

I am also in debt to all the professionals who helped teach me how to put a book together: my agent, Chris Tomasino; my attorney, Linda Stoick; and my editor at Hyperion, Jennifer Lang.

I also owe a debt of gratitude to many people at Charles Schwab, the company where I have been perfecting my own sense of balance since 1982. I thank my bosses, Chuck Schwab and Dave Pottruck, who let me experiment with my ideas amongst the Schwab employees and then allowed me to take a year off in order to put those ideas on paper. I was blessed with having Sandy Friedman as my assistant; she always supported me perfectly as I was trying to work at a job and a book simultaneously. And I would be remiss not to mention my co-workers who allowed me to interview them about their home and family lives.

Finally, I want to acknowledge my family. My husband and children have had to do with less of me as I have been writing. Their patience and love sustains me always.

Prologue

Everything has been figured out except how to live.
Jean-Paul Sartre

Where are you right now? Standing in a bookstore aisle during your lunch break? Crowded on a bus or subway on your daily commute? Collapsed in your bed, trying to read and unwind a bit after an exhausting day? Probably you don't have a lot of time for reading. In fact, you may feel like you don't have enough time for anything, particularly if it isn't job related. And you are hoping that somehow, this book can help you find more time in your life for what you enjoy.

I wrote this book for people like you, and people like me, who struggle with the constant time pressures in today's society. We all have jobs, commutes, and errands that seem endless. Added to that, most of us have family responsibilities, some of which are pleasurable and some of which, frankly, are not. But no matter, they all need to be done. Then there is the question, when do we ever get time for ourselves? Time to sleep late or read poetry or just do what we want? Our lament is a common one, which is rising across the country: "Please, I need to find more time."

Sadly, the answer that many of us reach is that there is no time. We feel caught in the relentless pressure of modern society, and, short of winning the lottery or hanging on until our retirement years, we have no way out. Since it seems we cannot have more time, we dream of achieving the next best thing: some balance, some more equal sharing of our time between our home lives and our work lives. On the surface, it is so little to ask for. We want to push back against the demands of our paying and nonpaying jobs and ask for some time to enjoy our loved ones and ourselves. Time to feel peace instead of frenzy, joy instead of tension, and appreciation instead of impatience.

Having a balanced life is not just a working women's issue, nor a working parents' issue. It is an issue that touches all of us, married, single, with or without children. As job pressures increase, as work environments seem less secure, as the world marketplace becomes more competitive, we respond by giving more of ourselves to our work. Not only do we labor long hours, but we also surround ourselves with electronic devices— pagers, cellular phones, laptop computers, e-mail, and voice mail—that give others the right to interrupt us at any moment with their digitally delivered demands.

Struggling to meet the ever-expanding expectations of the workplace, we end up starving our souls. And when our souls are starved, we can no longer nourish our work, our bodies, or the people who rely on us. We have nothing left to give.

The purpose of this book is to show you a way out. It will give you ways to examine the life you are living and show you how to make the changes you need to make you happier. This book isn't a sociological or academic study. The ideas are ones that I learned during my own thirteen-year search for balance. Some come from people I have worked with, some from friends, some from books, and some from people who've attended the seminars that I teach on having a balanced life. This book summarizes all those lessons for you, so you can create the life that is closer to what you want for yourself.

This book cannot change your life; only you can do that. But what this book can do is hold up a mirror so that you can see how you react to the world and pressures around you. With that vision, you can decide to make the changes you want to create the life you'd rather live.

Why Is It So Hard to Have a Balanced Life, Anyway?

WHERE TO FIND TIME

The animals in the kingdom get together to complain about the human beings. "They take my wool," bleats the sheep. "And then I feel cold when the night comes."

"They take my eggs," clucks the hen. "I will never have a brood of chickens."

"They take my milk," lows the cow, "without even bothering to ask."

Then the snail speaks up. "I have what humans want more than anything else but they can't take it from me. I have time."

Since you can't get time from the snail, where will you find it?

Why do we have to struggle to have balance in our lives? What has changed in the last decades that makes it so hard to be comfortable with our work and happy in our home life? Is it the workplace that has changed, growing so competitive that workaholism is considered a virtue? Or have our expectations changed? Do we believe the promise "you can have it all" when in fact no generation in history has ever enjoyed that privilege?

Why We Search for Balance

There can be no happiness if the things we believe in
are different from the things we do.
Freya Stark

Having balance between our work life and our home life is so desirable and reasonable, we can't accept the notion that it is unobtainable. By building balance, you grant yourself the freedom to express yourself as a whole person, through your job, in relationships, in your hobbies and passions. You have more time to nurture the important interests in your life, allowing you to create the "you" you have always wanted to be.

The formula for having a balanced life appears simple: work less and spend more time doing what you enjoy. Unfortunately, in our everyday lives this formula seems as remote and inapplicable as Einstein's equation for relativity. Intellectually, we know we have to cut down on the time we spend at work in order to become who we want to be, but we don't know how to make it happen. We worry about creating a threat to our jobs or careers. The ethics of our society celebrate the hard worker. To say "I don't want to work so much" seems immoral. Our parents and teachers and bosses and clients encourage us to strive harder, to work longer, and to do more. To buck this trend and admit that you want to work less implies there's something wrong with you. You are lazy or maybe uncommitted. To confess to your boss that you want to work fewer hours certainly sounds like the end of a previously promising career.

The Challenge of Finding Your Balance

*Now here, you see, it takes all the running you can do to keep in the
same place. If you want to get somewhere else, you must run
at least twice as fast as that.*
The White Queen (Lewis Carroll)

I can't tell you that it is easy to create a balanced life. Nor is it
easy to maintain it. In fact, at times living with balance in your
life can be more tiring than a unidimensional existence. When
I was working full time and mothering two small children, I
was always bone tired. I saw myself as an overworked pack-
horse, scrambling up a rocky mountainside with a huge load
on each side of the saddle. Balanced, yes, but also overburdened. Many days I felt like I had two full-time jobs, one with
my family and the other with my work.

Despite its exhausting connotations, the metaphor of two
full-time jobs became very useful for defining why I had to
have balance in my life. The hours for my for-pay job were
from 8 A.M. to 5:30 P.M. There were a certain set of responsibilities and a number of people who depended on me. I had to
be resourceful, reliable, and energetic. It was a job I wanted to
do. I would then commute to my home job, where the hours
were from 6:30 P.M. until 7 A.M. There were a certain set of
responsibilities and a number of people who depended on me.
I had to be resourceful, reliable, and energetic. This was
another job I wanted to do. Occasionally, I might long to
spend more hours at one job or another, but the twofold commitment never went away. Unyielding responsibilities and
anticipating individuals waited at either end of the commute.
I had to get myself there to do what was expected.

Managing Multiple Demands

We should consider every day lost in which we have not
danced at least once.
Friedrich Nietzsche

While battling my own balance issues I became more aware of the struggles of others. I observed many people who were stretched thin as rubber bands as they labored to meet home and work obligations. I saw others who had no lives outside of their jobs. But I also watched people who manage to keep aloft the various spinning plates of their home and work lives. They are clear in what they value and it isn't restricted to work. They know how to set limits. And they spend what time they have very wisely.

Despite their commonality in juggling the numerous demands placed before them, these people had very little in common. Some were highly placed in the business world; others were hourly workers. Some were long-standing corporate citizens, entrenched in the benefits of 401K plans and company-provided health insurance. Others were freelancers and consultants, relying on their own competence for the next assignment. They taught me that work/life balance does not come as a part of an organizational structure. Instead, it is a matter of understanding your own priorities and sticking to them, despite the pressures the outside world might apply.

Here are some people who are typical of those who have a balanced lifestyle. The first is a woman who works as an administrative assistant in a large company. She talks about how she divides her dedication between her job and her outside life:

At work, it's my job to be sure that my boss's life goes smoothly. On the other hand, my husband's career is in sales and that means we go to conferences and conventions three or four times a year. He entertains his clients at these events and since his client's spouses are usually there, I need to go along, too. I always tell my boss way in advance when I'll be gone and I double-check everything to make sure there are no hiccups while I am away. So far, there has never been a problem.

I also like to keep myself in shape. I work out at a gym for a couple of hours at lunch several times a week and make up the work hours by coming in early in the morning or working late in the evening. Some managers would balk at my constraints—they want assistants who guard their door like a sentry from 9 to 5 every day. But I found there are other bosses—like mine—who are comfortable with more flexible schedules and delighted to have someone like me work for them.

This next woman has climbed to the position of a division president, despite the focus she places on her family life:

I decided in high school that I wanted to have balance in my life. I wasn't going to drop dead of a heart attack some day. Over the years I've gotten really good at my techniques— I've had to, with a husband, two little kids, and my job. I set priorities and make sure I work on the important stuff that only I can do. Everything else I delegate, though I try to be careful to match the assignments to the person so they can get what they want, too. And I am a devotee of long-term planning—I can't stand fire drills. I like to be on the

*road going home by 5:45, and office crises don't let me do
that.*

*I've made trade-offs to get where I am though I don't trade
off my family. I neglect myself sometimes—I'm up at 5:30 in
the morning doing e-mail, I don't work out enough, and never
have any leisure time. Still I can't say I've compromised anything I really care about.*

The third example is a man who left the corporate world to
find the balance he desired:

*I had been working for a computer manufacturer and had a
very prestigious job there. But I got tired of sixty-hour workweeks and decided I had to do something else. So I quit. I
don't have the security of a steady job anymore, so I have to
be more careful about my finances. Plus I've simplified my
lifestyle and bought a cheaper car. But I can't tell you how
much happier I am! I spend half my time consulting for my old
firm but the best part of my life is restoring and then reselling
antique furniture. That's my true passion and now I have the
time to pursue it.*

These examples paint a picture of people who have built
balance into their lives. They devote time to those interests
outside of work that are important to them. They're clear with
themselves and others about the choices they are making.
They all have a certain confidence that they'll be successful in
their chosen field. In short, they know what they want from
life and how to go about getting it.

Creating Balance in Your Life

The one fact I would cry from every housetop is this:
The good life is waiting for us here and now.
B. F. Skinner

Can anyone create a balanced life for him- or herself? I believe most people can. The first step requires that you turn your attention from the "outer-directed" world to the "inner-directed" world. Instead of focusing exclusively on accomplishments that others acclaim, you need to concentrate on what will make you a happier and more authentic person. Focusing on those inner fundamental goals will force you to reorder your priorities. As you relearn what is truly important on your personal scorecard, you'll find it easier to turn from the world that reveres workaholics and enter the world that honors self-reflection and balance.

As you approach this new world, you may discover that no one but you cares if you get there. Your family wants you to spend more time with them. Your boss wants you to spend more time at work. Neither faction aspires for equilibrium, only for more of your time. At any point there'll be only one voice telling you to find some balance, and that'll be the tiny one inside your heart. Meanwhile there are dozens of others, your boss, colleagues, and customers, telling you to keep your head down, your brow furrowed, and work, work, work.

The intent of this book is to amplify your inner voice—to make it so strong and reasoned that you listen to yourself, accept your own wisdom, and create each day to your own specifications. As you do this, you might find you no longer conform to the standards of many co-workers and associates.

Like a Buddhist in the Bible Belt or a Democrat on Wall Street, you may have to learn to live with people whose value systems differ from your own. This is another step in having a balanced life: you have to create enough self-confidence to play the part of the rebel occasionally, albeit a harmless one who is actually practicing the lifestyle that many people yearn for.

Changing the Way You Think About Work

It's true hard work never killed anybody, but I figure
why take the chance?
Ronald Reagan

In addition to clarifying what's important to you, to improve the balance in your life, you need to redefine some of your beliefs about work. For many people the paradigm, or rules and regulations, that governs the relationship between their work and home lives goes something like this:

The Traditional Rules of Work
- Rule 1: Your boss and the responsibilities of your job control the number of hours you have to be at work.
- Rule 2: If you make the decision to spend more time on your home life instead of your work life, you will have a less rewarding career.
- Rule 3: Because there is never enough time to accomplish everything, you are forced to neglect some things that are important.

Creating a balanced life requires challenging those old rules and being willing to accept new notions that may or may not be comfortable to you. These new notions may seem Pollyanna-ish at first, but people who have balanced lives know they're true. After all, they apply them to their advantage every day.

The New Notions of Work
- Notion 1: You choose how you spend your time.
- Notion 2: You can make choices that favor your home life and still enjoy a rewarding career.
- Notion 3: You have enough time to do everything that is truly important to you.

There are at least two situations where Rule 1—your boss and the responsibilities of your job control the number of hours you have to be at work—may apply. If you are an hourly employee subject to strict overtime and scheduling policies, Traditional Rule 1 definitely affects you. Rule 1 might also hold true if you work in professions that deal with actual emergency situations, either medical, technological, or in law enforcement. If you are in one of these types of jobs, some of the advice in this book isn't relevant to your situation. That being said, New Notion 1 does applies to you—you can choose to find another job that offers you more flexibility (more on changing jobs in Chapter 12).

Once you accept the first new notion that you choose how you spend your time and not your boss or an intangible set of responsibilities, a new sense of freedom will enter your life. Hour by hour, day by day, you'll discover that the steering wheel is in your hands, the control panel is at your fingertips, the accelerator and brake are at your feet. You may decide to work as many hours as you ever did, but since it's your choice you feel empowered rather than enslaved. On the other hand, you may want to work fewer hours while still fulfilling all your responsibilities. In the second part of this book, you'll learn that there are many ways to meet your obligations without having to spend so many hours on them. Honing this skill frees you to make many different choices about how you spend your priceless time.

A bit of faith is required to believe in the second new notion of work, that you can make choices which favor your home life and still enjoy a rewarding career. Much of this book is devoted to teaching you how to make this happen. You'll learn that the same techniques which allow you to create more balance in your life also make you more resourceful and effective in any endeavor you choose, consequently improving your chances for success on the job.

The third new notion is to realize that you have enough time to do everything that is important to you. The secret here is to be discriminating about what you consider important. This means reducing the conflicting priorities that populate your life today and then zeroing in on the unadulterated essentials. You'll discard activities that absorb time but give meager returns. Instead, you'll be defining the life you want to live and then using your time to make it a reality.

At first, each of these new notions may be difficult to accept wholeheartedly. However, over time you'll see that they work. Having talked with hundreds of people about how they've achieved balance, I've learned that they all apply these new notions to their lives in one form or another. By changing the rules they play by, people with balance have changed the game.

Using This Book

How many shrinks does it take to change a lightbulb? It only takes
one, but the lightbulb has to really want to change.
Anonymous

This book is divided into four parts, each designed to show you how to change your work patterns and find more balance in your life. The first part helps you understand yourself better. In it, you explore what's truly important to you. You'll also learn what motivates you—what internal drivers like guilt or ambition or other people's expectations might be preventing you from finding the balance you want. Part 2 explains how to make the changes you need to create a balanced life. It includes approaches to time management and how you can get your boss, customers, and co-workers to accept your need for balance. The third part describes particular situations that are common but may not apply to everyone. There is a chapter that deals specifically with the challenges faced by working parents, as well as one which discusses how to find balance if you are single and childless. This part of the book also discusses how to change jobs so you can keep or improve your balance. Part 4 talks about activities that will help you increase the balance in your life this year and in the years to come.

Within each chapter, I use anecdotes from various people who, like you, face conflicts between their work lives and their home lives. Some of these people attended the Balanced Life courses that I taught, others were present at one of my lectures, and some told me their thoughts during a conversation or through e-mail. I have taken a few liberties as I retell these people's stories. I've paraphrased many conversations and have edited some of the e-mails I've received for clarity and brevity. Occasionally when I describe who's telling the tale, I've modified a job title or switched genders. But I have tried never to change the essence of these anecdotes. My hope is that these people's experiences, feelings, and knowledge will convince you that you too can create the balance you seek.

Each chapter in the book ends with a series of exercises that let you practice what I've been preaching. Taking the time to complete the exercises makes having a balanced life more than just an intellectual activity. They help you build the self-awareness you need to question and sometimes reject the rules and values that our overworked society proclaims. In fact, if you want more balance in your life and have extremely limited time, you're probably better off doing the exercises and only skimming the chapters. Everyone knows you can't learn to ride a bicycle without climbing on. Even if you know where to put your hands and feet, you'll never get the right balance. Similarly, if you want balance in your daily life, you have to get out there and try. The exercises encourage you to develop the self-knowledge and reflection you'll need.

No matter what you do, however, it is impossible for anyone to have a life that is always perfectly balanced between home and work. My intent is that this book will help you obtain *more* balance. But as circumstances change, as "s**t happens," your life will be thrown out of balance for some period of time. With luck, that time will be short and you'll soon return to a life which more accurately reflects who you are and who you want to be. But no matter what life presents you, this book will have served its purpose if it helps you discard or even modify a workaholic lifestyle and create a better life for yourself and those who care about you.

Exploration Exercises

Looking in the Mirror

Take out a piece of white paper, about 8½ by 11. Get a pencil or pen and some colored markers if you have any. Draw an old-fashioned hanging scale, like the ones held by the statues of justice. Label one side "home life" and the other side "work life." Show how the scales are out of balance. If you think your work life far outweighs your home life, draw that side lower down. If you think they are close, draw them that way.

Next, put your pencil down and take two or three deep breaths. Close your eyes and imagine what your home life would be like if you had more time. What would you add? More exercise, more time with friends, more time with your family? Once you have a mental picture, draw symbols of what you want or write down the words and draw arrows from them into the home-life side of your scale.

Take another series of deep breaths and imagine seeing your work life as if it were on a video. What scenes would you erase? The boring meetings, the overly demanding co-worker, the make-work projects, the stress? Depict those on the work-life side of your picture with arrows showing they are going out of the scale.

Your objective as you continue to work through this book is to make this sketch come true. Tuck your picture into this book so as new ideas come to you, they can be added to your drawing.

Commute Questions

(These questions are for you to ponder when you are commuting, waiting in line, etc. Think of them as directed daydreams.)

Think about the first new notion of work: "You choose how you spend your time." Think about your workday, either the one you are commuting to or the one you're just leaving from, and ask yourself which are your least favorite activities or events. Were those images included when you drew your scale? What would it take for you to avoid or minimize similar activities or events in the days to come? If those activities are important, is there some way they could get done without you having to do them? If you chose not to participate in these unrewarding events, how much of a difference would it make to you or your job six months from now?

Action Step
Write down how you would complete this thought: *To me, having a balanced life means* . . . (If you are interested in how other people finished this thought, look for the quote at the end of each chapter.)

> To me, having a balanced life means loving what you do and doing what you love in everything you do.
>
> A 41-year-old technologist and aspiring professional angler

Part 1:

LOOKING INWARD

Would you sell the colors of your sunset

and the fragrance

Of your flowers, and the passionate

wonder of your forest

For a creed that will not let you dance?

Helene Johnson

2

Identifying What Is Important to You

COMING UP FOR AIR

A Zen student comes to his master and complains that he can't concentrate on his meditation exercises. "Think of your breath," says the master. "Concentrate on that."

"But my breathing is so uninteresting," says the student. "Can't you give me another assignment?"

With that, the master seizes the student and forces his head into a tub of water. The student struggles, but the master doesn't let him up until he is half drowned.

"Now," says the master. "Is breathing still so uninteresting?"

*What is there in your life that is important to you and yet you take it
for granted? Does someone have to deprive you of that important
aspect of your life in order for you to appreciate it?*

Do you know how to answer the question, "What is important to you?" Can you say which is more important to you, your home life or your work life? Most people state that their home lives are more important. But that's not always how we act.

Imagine yourself in the following situation. How would you handle it?

It's time to go. Your briefcase is packed. You've made a commitment to be somewhere in thirty minutes. You'll just make it if you leave now. Unexpectedly, someone comes up to you and says he has an important issue he wants to discuss with you. Could you take just a few minutes to talk?

If you imagined yourself in a work setting and are like most conscientious employees, you would take those few moments to talk, even if it made you late. Now imagine yourself in this situation:

You're leaving for work in the morning. You have a meeting in thirty minutes. You'll just make it if you leave now. Unexpectedly, your spouse or child comes up to you and says he or she has an important issue to discuss. Can you talk about it now?

What would you do? Most people see themselves racing right out the door. They have to get to work! Nothing could be so important that it couldn't wait until the evening.

So why does this dichotomy exist? Why do we put a higher importance on our work colleagues' issues than on our families' issues?

Part of the answer is that our families let us behave badly and yet still accept us. Bosses are neither so loving nor forgiving. But just because we can shortchange our home lives doesn't mean we should. Each time we slight our home lives, we are acting out of harmony with a core value. These small incidents accumulate and cause us to feel stressed, guilty, and not in control of our own lives. We know we want to be true to our values, but somehow too many tiny decisions lead us astray.

When Priorities Conflict

What you do speaks so loud that I cannot hear what you say.
Ralph Waldo Emerson

The sad fact is that for many people, work demands are always more compelling than those of their home lives. The arguments for favoring your work life over your home life are very specific: "I need the paycheck." "I need the raise." "I need the promotion." "I have responsibilities at work." All this is probably true. But don't you also need loving relationships, a home that brings you serenity, and the time to nurture your physical and spiritual self? Of course you do, and these aspects of your life have as much of a right to demand your time as your boss does.

But how do you convince yourself that it's all right to turn down a work request in order to spend more time on your home life? Returning to our earlier example, how do you say "No" to a colleague when you're trying to be home in time for dinner or to get to the gym for your volleyball game? One key is to have a very clear picture of your personal priorities, those that matter to you as much as your work. Your work priorities are probably clear to you already. When you're at work, there tends to be reinforcement as to why your job is important and what goals you are meant to accomplish. You have a sense of what success looks like. But what is success for you in your home life? What do you want to achieve? Just what in your home life is important to you?

Expanding the Definition of Success

Getting what you go after is success; but liking it while
you are getting it is happiness.
Bertha Damon

Too often in our society, the term *success* connotes career success. But by limiting the definition that way, we cheat ourselves. Career success can be very rewarding, not only financially but also for our psyches. But confining the definition of success to the marketplace overshadows the value of success in the rest of our lives. Assume for a moment that you will achieve whatever level of career success you want in your life. What else do you want to accomplish before you die? How do you want to be remembered and by whom? Just what kind of a person do you want to be?

Very few people spend time thinking about what is truly important to them other than their work. This is such a great loss. Identifying your priorities is like paging through a scrapbook of fondly remembered times. Each image brings a smile of recognition and a sense of belonging. Once you reacquaint yourself with your core values, you'll always have your guiding stars, even during the darkest times.

But how do you identify your particular priorities, whether they're related to home or to work? I'm not talking about the expectations that others have for you, but what you want for yourself, your Personal Priorities. The following exercise gives you the opportunity to identify those Personal Priorities, to understand what is truly important to you both in your work life and your home life. These Priorities shouldn't seem new to you. Most probably you have valued them for years and will continue to treasure them for years to come.

An Exercise to Discover Your Priorities

Carefully observe what way your heart draws you and then choose that way with all your strength.
Hasidic Proverb

Usually the exercises that help you build a balanced life come at the end of each chapter, but this particular exercise is so crucial and takes so little time that I want you to do it now. Be somewhere you can concentrate for ten to fifteen minutes. You will need a pencil or pen and fifteen to twenty index cards (you can also use the back of business cards or small pieces of notepaper). Having quiet music in the background is helpful, too. Set aside your immediate concerns for a while and be prepared to think about yourself and what you want from your life.

Take a look at the list of phrases that follow. Which ones are important to you, in either your home or your work life?

As you see phrases that appeal to you, copy each down individually on a card or small piece of paper. Now sort through those and create a pile limited to the *five* that are most important to you. That's right, choose only five. If you have trouble limiting yourself, you can stretch the rules and create subcategories. For instance, you might choose "Having a close family" as the main category and include "Parenting wisely" and "Connecting, caring, relating to others" as a part of it. If you're still having difficulties, then focus on what is most important for you in the next year or two.

Being creative	Having personal freedom	Having lots of fun
Enjoying a wonderful leisure life	Enjoying my hobbies	Having time alone
Being physically active	Being healthy	Being physically attractive
Having good self-esteem	Using my talents and skills	Being a whole person
Following my heart's desire	Being a weaver of my own cloth	Seeking excitement and adventure
Experiencing something new	Seeing the world	Learning new things
Being financially independent	Getting to the top	Achieving goals
Being satisfied with my career	Having influence	Believing my work counts
Protecting the environment	Making the world a better place	Giving to my community
Making a difference	Practicing my faith	Connecting with all things
Having a close family	Parenting wisely	Being committed to a life partner
Connecting, caring, relating to others	Having good friends/ being a good friend	Creating a home
Trusting powers beyond myself	Developing my spirituality	Believing my life counts
Appreciating the beauty around me	Being visionary	Finding inner wisdom
Experiencing peace within me	Simplifying my life	Living in the moment
Being able to forgive	Being filled with love and kindness	Being generous to others
Aging gracefully	Leaving a legacy	Enjoying retirement

Limiting your number of Personal Priorities to five may seem arbitrary, but it actually serves a critical purpose. Time is limited. You have too much going on already—that's why you bought this book. Limiting yourself to a reasonable number of priorities makes each more likely to happen. Besides, as you limit yourself to five, you'll force yourself to make those hard choices about what does matter to you. The choices you make might surprise you, as they did this woman:

I had been completely freaked out and depressed about having neither a social life nor time to catch up with close friends for the last two years. The Personal Priority exercise helped me realize those aren't my most important objectives now, though they may become the most important later. When they do become most important, then I'll devote the time to them.

The process of committing to your life's most meaningful priorities releases you from the burden of having too many obligations. This woman felt guilty and stressed because she didn't have the time to keep up with her friends. By realizing that other aspects of her life were more important, she could let go of those conflicting expectations of herself, storing them in the upper attic of her consciousness where they'll wait until she's ready to bring them down again.

How Priorities Lead to Balance

There is a part of every living thing that wants to become itself.
Ellen Bass

For most people, this Personal Priority exercise opens the way to finding the balance they want in their lives. Rather than trying to do everything and finding their schedules and their lives overburdened with commitments, they are able to concentrate on their own Priorities. For example, an office worker writes,

Having Personal Priorities has definitely helped. I carry my list with me at all times in my Day-Timer. Occasionally, after

*I've been at work for many hours, I'll be flipping through my
Day-Timer and see my list of Priorities. I'll glance through
them and realize that work is only one of the many important
aspects of my life. Not only will I finish up and go home, but
I'm able to do it without any guilt! It's great to have that
reminder at my fingertips whenever I need it.*

Creating a way to be reminded of your Priorities makes
them even more useful to you. Write them in your Day-Timer
or post them on your mirror or computer screen. Put them in
your wallet or jewelry box—anywhere you will see them daily.
Create mental images as well. As you get into your car, see
your priorities as the four tires and the steering wheel, each
essential to getting you from here to there. If you are a journal writer, make a note each day of how you're true to your
Priorities.

Integrating reminders of your Personal Priorities into your
daily life makes them more tangible. As you make choices
about how to spend your time, they're there to help you. As
you think about your day, they remind you of what's important. Listen to how this young man used the insights he had
gained from identifying his Personal Priorities:

*I finally narrowed it down to five Priorities: "Developing my
spirituality," "Having a close family," "Being satisfied with
my career," "Being healthy," and "Being visionary." I placed
the list in the foremost compartment of my wallet. That way
every time I open it I'm reminded of the commitment I have
made to myself.*

*My commute is thirty to forty minutes. The first ten min-
utes of this I think about my Priorities and decide how I can
apply them to my day. Even if it's something quick (saying*

a prayer, calling my wife for no reason other than to say "I love you," not eating that Snickers bar in the afternoon), it is one more step in the journey and my work time doesn't suffer!

You can see how identifying your Priorities enhances your home life and renews your sense of balance, but you may not realize there are other benefits as well. Knowing your Priorities can also make your work life more rewarding. A human resource specialist who attended one of my workshops wrote to say,

The exercise on Personal Priorities reminded me of what fuels my soul. That, in turn, fuels my contributions to the company I work for. If my soul is undernourished, sooner or later so will be my contributions.

Too often people assume that adding balance to their lives will lessen their work contributions. But frequently, respecting all that's important to you rejuvenates your entire being, generating more energy for both your work life and your home life. The exercise on Personal Priorities has helped many people understand this paradox. See if it doesn't work for you as well.

Putting Your Time Where It Matters Most

It is not how much we have, but how much we enjoy,
that makes happiness.
Charles H. Spurgeon

With the understanding of what's truly important to you comes the confidence to choose the best way to spend your time. You'll find that others' opinions count for less. No longer will you let your own desires become buried under the avalanche of other people's expectations. You'll strike a better balance, like this manager did:

> One of my Priorities is "Making a difference." I currently serve on the board of an educational nonprofit. The founder of the nonprofit was recently in town from New York and asked to have me and others attend a variety of meetings with him to try to enlist more financial support. I had just started a new job and I think I would have been much more reluctant to take several hours off if I hadn't recently done the Priority exercise. When I took a step back, I realized that it would "make a much bigger difference" to get some funding to help disadvantaged kids than to work a few more hours.

As you struggle to decide whether to devote your precious hours to work or another Priority, remember your ultimate objective—to be a success in life, not just at your job. At the end of your life, you won't be remembered for how you earned your money, but for how you spent your time.

Learning There's Less to Worry About

The art of being wise is the art of knowing what to overlook.
William James

Whenever you nurture your Personal Priorities, you're reminding yourself that yes, you do have control over your life. While unpredictable or unpleasant events will still sweep in, once you're aware of your Priorities, you can discriminate more easily between what's essential and what's incidental to your well-being.

This sales representative relates how knowing her Personal Priorities lowered the stress in her life:

> *Having a list of my Personal Priorities helps me focus on what's important. If I'm feeling anxious about something, I look at my list. If whatever is bothering me isn't on the list, I say, "How important can it be?" If it is on the list, I look for a way to reduce the stress by focusing on what I can do to make what is important to me less stressful.*

Identifying your Personal Priorities will help you understand that you have the power to decide which problems are worth your time. If something related to your Priorities is going awry, then it deserves your attention. However, if the issue doesn't concern one of your top five, put your anxiety into its appropriate context. Turn your attention back to the aspects of your life that are important. The more you focus on what really matters to you, the less time you'll have for worries.

Living Your Priorities

The man (or woman) is a success who has lived well, laughed often, and loved much.
Robert Louis Stevenson

Identifying your Priorities is the first step toward creating a balanced life. The second is discovering enough motivation to change your current habits. Different triggers cause people to change their patterns and make a balanced life a priority.

Some people are motivated by a loss. Who doesn't think about personal life choices while attending a funeral, especially if the deceased was a friend close in age? Joyous occasions also induce change. No parent can hold a wrinkled newborn and not resolve to be there for him or her always. (Of course, more frequently it's not the labor room resolutions but the reality of an infant—inadequate sleep, incessant earaches, or child-care catastrophes—that forces a change in lifestyle.)

Other times the motivation for change comes from appreciating other people's experiences. I recently heard the story of a nurse who worked with cancer patients. "What do you really want to do with your life?" they would ask her. "Spend more time outdoors," was her answer. "Then do it," they urged, for having cancer had taught them what was truly important. The nurse listened to their advice and quit to return to her family farm.

Most of us don't have to leave our jobs to achieve what is truly important to us. The vast majority of people can continue in their current work situation and still add more of what's important to their lives. You have taken the crucial first step by identifying your Personal Priorities. Now you've done that, the next step is to build the motivation and time management skills to pursue the five Priorities you have chosen.

Exploration Exercise

Looking in the Mirror
1. For each of your five Personal Priorities, write down what it means to you. For example, if you chose "Being financially independent," does that mean you want to be able to retire

comfortably when you are 55, or do you have a set dollar amount you want to acquire? Or, if you chose "Having a close family," does that mean just your nuclear family, or does it include the entire clan?

2. What can you do to make your Personal Priorities part of your daily life? For each Priority, list as many activities as you can think of that could be done in ten minutes, in an hour, or even while waiting in line or on your commute.

3. As you think about your Personal Priorities, ask yourself the following questions:

   - Which Priority have you valued the longest and which is relatively new?
   - Is one or two of your Priorities more important than the others? Less important?
   - Which Priority is most neglected in your life right now?
   - Into which Priority, if any, do you want to put the most energy right now?

4. Review the balance scales you drew for the exercise in Chapter 1. Are your Personal Priorities represented? If not, include them on either the work side or the home side of your scales.

Commute Questions
(*These questions are for you to ponder when you are commuting, waiting in line, etc. Think of them as directed daydreams.*)
Once you have narrowed down your Personal Priorities, it makes it easier to put them into practice. As you are going to work in the morning, think of one or two things you might do during the day that would contribute to your sense of developing your Priorities. On the way home, think about what you did do and congratulate yourself, no matter how small the effort.

Action Step

Take a typical workday and see if you can design in activities for some or all of your Personal Priorities. Then try to do it and see how close you come. Here are a few examples:

MY FIVE PERSONAL PRIORITIES	ACTIVITY
1. Being commited to a life partner	On my commute, I will think about how we could get away for a night, just the two of us.
2. Being physically active	Instead of hitting the snooze button, I will get up and go for a quick jog in the morning.
3. Being satisfied with my career	I will schedule time with my boss to talk about how I can expand my responsibilities.
4. Being financially independent	Instead of working through lunch hour, I will calculate how much money a month I can devote to long-term savings.
5. Parenting wisely	When I put my children to bed tonight, I will tell them why I'm proud of them.

MY FIVE PERSONAL PRIORITIES	ACTIVITY
1. Developing my spirituality	Before going to bed, I will take a moment to be grateful for all my blessings.
2. Seeing the world	During lunch hour, I will browse the travel section of a nearby bookstore.
3. Giving to my community	I will attend my church's fund-raising meeting this evening.
4. Having good friends/being a good friend	I will write an e-mail to my friend who lives out of state just to say hello.
5. Appreciating the beauty around me	Instead of rushing to the bus stop in the morning, I will take a moment to admire the morning sky.

> To me, having a balanced life—more now than ever before—means knowing what my priorities are, and dedicating myself to them.
>
> A mother and manager who decided to leave the fast track in order to spend more time with her young children.

Understanding What Motivates You

PLEASING EVERYONE, PLEASING NO ONE

A farmer and his son are leading their donkey to market where they plan to sell the beast. As they're walking, a woman sees them and starts laughing. "Look at those fools, walking beside their donkey when they could ride."

Upon hearing this, the man tells his son to ride the donkey. The next person they see grunts in disgust. "That boy has no respect for his elders. Why does he ride and his poor father has to walk?" With that, the father tells the son to get down and let him ride.

Two young women see them approach. "What a selfish man," they scold. "Making his poor young son walk while he rides." The father, not knowing what to do, pulls his son up on the donkey with him and they both ride.

The next man who passes rolls his eyes at the sight. "Those people have no respect for animals. That poor donkey is nearly lame from carrying all that weight. Those two should be carrying the donkey, instead of the other way around."

Puzzled but eager to please, the farmer tries to pick up the donkey in his arms. With that the donkey panics, kicks the man, and runs off, never to return.

How much do the opinions of others shape your behavior?

Now that you have rediscovered your Personal Priorities, it is time to ask yourself why you don't devote more time to all those important and wonderful aspects of your life. Whether you want to admit it or not, you are making choices. If "Creating a home" is important to you, yet you haven't been home in the daylight hours for months, then something is not right. If "Travel and see the world" is a priority and your longest vacation in the last year was to take three days to visit your parents, you have to ask yourself why.

Your first reaction may be to blame your work environment, and in some cases that's appropriate. But I would speculate in many cases, it is you and not your boss who is making the decision about how much time you spend at the office. In other words, it's not the work, it's how you respond to the demands of the work. As a broker who attended one of my seminars succinctly stated, "My supervisor doesn't get in the way of balance—I do."

Many people aren't even aware of why they spend so long on the job, as demonstrated by this computer programmer who didn't understand what compelled him to work so many hours:

I used to think that it was my boss who made me work late, but she changed jobs a couple of weeks ago and I don't have a supervisor now. The weird thing is, I still work long hours. Even though there is nothing urgent happening these days, I didn't go home until after 7 last night. I thought about leaving earlier, but somehow it didn't feel right. It was then I realized that I am the one who is making me work all those hours. I had been getting angry with my boss for something she didn't even do.

What Makes You Work Such Long Hours?

If I am not for myself, then who will be?
Talmud

Hopefully, one of the reasons you work so hard is that you love your job. But since you also like spending time on your Personal Priorities, what are the motivators that drive you away from a life that is balanced and into a life of long workdays? While this is certainly not an exhaustive list, the major motivating forces I've observed in others and myself are (1) money (no surprise!), (2) the need for approval, (3) peer pressure, (4) a sense of obligation to oneself or others, (5) the desire to win, and (6) the need for power and control.

How many of these push your buttons? Read the following descriptions and see which of them might be keeping you from having the balance you want in your life.

Money   Increasing your take-home pay means a great deal to you, perhaps as much on a symbolic level as on a financial level. This project manager acknowledges the effect money has on his decisions:

> I confess; I am motivated by money. I'm caught up in the web of thinking that I need to work really hard to be able to provide the (best) things I want for my child, to live the way I want to, to satisfy my own (or is it my family's?) sense of pride.

The Need for Approval   You strive for the praise or admiration of others and feel terrible if there is any perceived or actual criticism. A legal assistant writes,

I am very motivated by the immediate response of others—I like to please and I feel guilty for just about anything you can think of! One of the things I'm working on is not being so motivated by the immediate demands, but trying to take a step back so I am not agreeing to everything all the time.

<u>Peer Pressure</u> The people around you or people you care about work long hours, so you feel you should, too. A business school graduate comments,

For me, the challenge in leading a balanced life has a lot to do with the "keeping up with the Joneses" syndrome. I especially find that when I get together with my friends from business school, it's requisite to talk about how busy we all are—how we are stretched so thinly we can't remember the last time we just watched the grass grow. Exercising? Forget it. Called Aunt Helen in Kansas? No way. It is almost absurd to me, but I find that I play right into it. In my peer group, it is perceived as failure if you work "normal" hours.

<u>Living Up to Expectations</u> You feel obliged to fulfill your own high expectations of yourself and can't bear the idea of coming up short. Or you feel a sense of deep obligation to someone and don't want to be a disappointment. This analyst realizes that both his father's expectations and his own motivate him:

I think I am largely driven (but I could be fooling myself) by my own expectations. These are usually the highest and thus make my life the most miserable/driven. However, I am also definitely tormented by a very clear awareness of my father's expectations and how I've chosen to do things my own way despite them.

Competition   Either you really love to win or you really hate to lose. You are equally motivated by big or small competitions. This salesperson describes how competition drives him:

I enjoy working in a competitive environment. It's exciting and gets my adrenaline going. I think that striving to be number one really brings out the best in me.

Desire for Power and Control   You feel as if you have to be the one who is in authority and setting the direction. You dislike being told what to do. This consultant describes her urge to increase her influence:

I think one of the reasons I am so ambitious is that I hate being told what to do. Frankly, most of the people I have worked for aren't as smart as I am. If working hard gives me a shot at having my boss's job, great.

Of course, none of us is motivated by only one force. Frequently a combination of stimuli swirls through our heads as we try to do what is right for ourselves and what is acceptable to others.

Understand Your Motivations

Know thyself? If I knew myself, I'd run away.
Johann von Goethe

It's extremely important for you to know what motivates you. It is the only way that you'll be able to change your habits so you have more balance. You need to pay less attention to what causes you to work long hours and focus more on what allows you to spend time on your home life.

When I examine myself, I see that my primary motivator is my insatiable desire for praise. I love it when people say nice things about me. Phrases like "Nice job" and "That's a good point" or "Don't you look great today" make me smile inside and out. One of the reasons I adore public speaking is that people clap for me at the end.

The shadow side of this motivator is my hypersensitivity to criticism. I can't bear to have people tell me I've done something wrong. Many years ago, I was a secretary at an ad agency and had to fill in for the telephone operator when she went to lunch. One day I left an important client on hold for five minutes (I had forgotten he was there), and one of the account executives stormed out of his office and yelled at me. I escaped, weeping, into the ladies' room and didn't regain my composure for almost an hour.

Luckily, I have a better grip on my emotions these days, but I still tend to tear up if I get reprimanded. Because of that, I'm highly motivated to never, ever mess up!

In addition to the influence praise and criticism have on me, money and competition also matter. To me, money is a scorecard and I detest earning less than someone who I think isn't as good as I am.

How does understanding what motivates me keep balance in my life? In the first place, I apply my energies to areas where I know I'll do well. Not only am I more apt to get the praise I crave, I'm also most efficient and effective when I do things I like. When I have to do tasks I don't do well, I quickly ask for help from my boss or a colleague so I won't be caught making a mistake. I put extra value on any compliments I get about keeping balance in my life. And whenever I get upset about not earning as much as one of my peers, I convince myself, with or without justification, that I have a richer family life than he or she does.

Prevent Others from Controlling Your Time

Comparing my insides to other people's outsides causes me problems.
Joan Rhode

Another reason to understand your motivation is to be able to resist other people's attempts to control your time. Effective managers and supervisors are highly skilled at getting people to change their behavior. They use any and all of the motivators I've described to get superior performance out of their workers. However, those of us who want balanced lives can't afford to have other people yanking on our leashes and making choices for us. Their priorities might not be our priorities. Therefore, we must resist the manipulations of these trained professionals. We have to impede their efforts by understanding our internal drivers better than they can.

Imagine yourself in a staff meeting and your boss starts praising Wally Workaholic for putting in 80-hour weeks for the last two months. She is obviously trying to encourage the rest of her team to work that many hours as well. Can you resist the pressure? To do so, you need a good sense of what motivators influence you as much as the boss's accolades. For example, as your boss drones on about Wally, you might be saying to yourself,

I know Wally chooses to work a lot of hours, but I have made a commitment to myself that my friends and my volunteer work are more important to me than hearing the boss's praise on a daily basis. I am not going to let someone else's value system control me. Besides, Wally wastes a lot of time on superficial stuff. I am much more effective than he is.

Private pep talks that reinforce your Personal Priorities and point out the flaws in other people's logic or character can be very useful in counterbalancing the approval given to the workaholic. Listen carefully to your inner voice and remind yourself that no one ever said creating a balanced life would be easy!

If you're lucky, just being aware of the motivators that control you can be enough to cause you to tweak your behavior. Other times it takes a combination of awareness, logic, and self-manipulation to reexert authority over those silent forces that keep you from a balanced life. While you will never be totally free of the motivations that compel you, there are ways to be less driven if you try some of the techniques described next.

Reduce Money's Influence

Money is all right but you have to waste a lot of time making it.
Anonymous

Are you motivated by money? Aren't we all? Money is important to each of us. It represents freedom, comfort, security, and power. It is a rare individual who doesn't long for at least one of those. Unfortunately, having a balanced life does not lead directly to creating a bulkier bank account. So if you are strongly motivated by money, over-time pay or the hope of an extra sales commission can be very alluring. So alluring, in fact, that your pledge to have a balanced life evaporates beneath the heat of monetary desire.

How to resist? The first weapon of resistance should be logic—how much money are you actually going to take home by working longer at this time? What Personal Priority are you giving up to get that money? Is the trade-off worth it? Why is that amount of money important to you?

The last question, why is that amount of money important to you, is key to understanding why money is such a significant motivator to you. Is the money going for essentials—rent, food, taxes, child care? Or is it going into longer range savings—an IRA or a down payment on a house?

Some people justify their quest for money by believing they need the funds to enhance their families' lifestyle, like buying a fancier car or going on special vacations. If this applies to you, you might ask your family if they like the choices you're making. It's possible that they'd rather see more of you than go to the Bahamas every winter. And if they do vote for the Bahamas over seeing you, how happy are you with that decision?

Other people chase after money for emotional as well as financial reasons. This software designer explains his situation:

> My efforts to make money have been directly connected to my desire to get to a place that no one thought possible for me. Also, there's a sense of pride wrapped up in there, too. It's one of those things about getting "legitimacy." My folks never made oodles of money. So I have been quietly ambitious over the years in order to get places they never got to—not to show them up, but to make them proud of me and to convince myself I could do it.

Think about why money is important to you and then compare it against your other Personal Priorities. Sometimes having money is relevant to your Priorities and sometimes it isn't. Weighing the relative importance of the money against your other Priorities can help you get a better grasp on how you want to be spending your time.

If money means a lot to you emotionally and you can't seem to make yourself work fewer hours, you might consider this trick. Decide that you are going to leave by a certain time, say 5:30 every Tuesday and Thursday. Then tell people, lots of people, that you will pay them each $5 if they see you in the office after 5:35 on those days. Make sure you have the cash in your wallet so you are paying out real money and not IOUs. Giving away those $5 bills will get painful fast and you'll be delighted to go home.

Don't Be Swayed by Praise

Great tranquillity of heart is his who cares for
neither praise nor blame.
Thomas à Kempis

One way to diminish the importance of work-related praise is to fill your life with good feelings from developing your other Personal Priorities. And if you start investing time in your Priorities, you might be surprised by how much more content you feel, like this young woman:

One of the things that I do is to make a real effort to call close friends who don't live nearby. I'm trying to focus on the people who really matter to me. This makes me feel so much better, which translates into better balance in every respect. If something at work doesn't go well, it just doesn't mean so much.

Another way to wean yourself off work-related praise is listen for any compliments related to your Personal Priorities. Imagine you have a praise quota in each of your Priorities and you have to fulfill your quota for each one. Praise from work may be nice, but you will also need someone commending you for "Being physically active" or for "Learning new things" or for "Being a whole person." Do you think anyone will even notice what you do outside of work? Of course they will. You might hear things like "You're so fit. I admire your energy." Or "I'm really impressed you're taking the time to learn Japanese." Or "You never let the little stuff at work bother you. You are really a well-rounded person." And if people don't say them to you enough, say them to yourself. No one is going to give you a plaque for being a balanced person, but they will admire you for it.

Release Yourself from Peer Pressure

I think the reward for conformity is that everyone
likes you except yourself.
Rita Mae Brown

Peer pressure is another motivator that drives people into ridiculous work schedules. Unable to set an individual course, some people find themselves working unnecessarily long hours just so they can feel as if they belong to the right gang. To avoid this, you have to disengage yourself from the crutch of groupthink and become comfortable being more of your own person.

Once again, your Personal Priorities can be a support for you. You know that each person in your peer group has a set of Personal Priorities that differ from yours. Your desires for your life are very special and unique. It's ludicrous to think that you should pattern your behavior after the actions of others. If you really believe and care about your own Personal Priorities, the appeal of the group's norms will diminish. You can start living on your own schedule, creating the life you want, and not feel bound by others' values.

Once he gained some perspective, this man was able to separate himself from the desire to keep in step with his associates:

I used to be very motivated by peer pressure. I would try to match my pace to the other guys just because they were work-ing at that level. But then I stepped back for a bit and saw that there is a life outside of work. Now if someone asks me why I'm coming in so late, I explain that I put in my eight to nine hours and this is the way I have shifted my schedule to ensure it.

Will breaking the norms of your peer group slow your advancement within the firm? Not necessarily. Many of the timesaving tips in Chapter 5 show how developing more balance in your life can actually help to *improve* your performance at work. Remember that the New Notion of Work says you can make choices that favor your home life and still enjoy a rewarding career. Why not be a leader within your peer group and prove it to be true?

Pay Less Attention to All Those Obligations

A man's conscience takes up more room than the rest of his insides.
Huck Finn (Mark Twain)

When we think we're not fulfilling our obligations to others or ourselves, we feel guilty. Guilt is one of the most powerful motivators there is. We all feel it. We all hate feeling it. We all respond to it. Few of us ever learn how to escape it. Which is not to say that guilt is bad. It serves a very useful role in society. It helps rein in our selfish and lawless instincts so we can live together in relative safety and harmony.

On the other hand, guilt is not always an appropriate emotion. Sometimes it interferes with having a balanced life because we can't tell the difference between guilt that is warranted and guilt that is unnecessary. R. D. Laing, the eminent psychologist, describes guilt this way: "True guilt is guilt at the obligation one owes to oneself to be oneself. False guilt is guilt felt at not being what other people feel one ought to be or assume that one is."

How do we tell the difference between true guilt and false guilt? In other words, when is guilt appropriate and when is it not? When I feel guilty, I test for inappropriate guilt by asking myself if I'm also berating myself for feeling guilty. If my internal voice pipes up with "I shouldn't feel guilty about this," I know I am suffering from inappropriate guilt.

For example, last summer when I backed out of my driveway too fast and scraped the car parked across the street, I felt guilty. I never asked myself if I should feel guilty or not. I was guilty; I should have felt guilty.

On the other hand, I also feel guilty when I'm curt with the telemarketers who call during dinner. As I rejoin my family at the table, I keep telling myself I shouldn't feel guilty. In that case, I've become the victim of inappropriate guilt.

Sometimes it is surprisingly difficult to distinguish between appropriate and inappropriate guilt. For example, people striving for balance often feel guilty about leaving work even after they have put in a full day:

> I work in a small office, and I used to (and still do sometimes) feel guilty even about leaving on time. I felt that because of all the firm has done for me, I owed "it" more than just my eight or nine hours a day. I'm finally realizing that I owe myself that time.

Although I would never counsel anyone to avoid appropriate guilt, I do advise everyone to try to overcome inappropriate guilt. To do this, it is useful to understand the nature of guilt. Guilt is frequently associated with resentment, a form of passive anger. What we feel as guilt can actually be anger over expectations we are not fulfilling. Sometimes these expectations can't be attributed to any one person. They aren't real but only projections of our own expectations. Sometimes the expectations come from a specific individual. This may make them real, but not necessarily realistic or reasonable. So the next time you feel guilty, go through this exercise and see if it helps:

Getting Over Guilt
- Whose expectations are you not meeting?
- Are they implicit or explicit?
- If they are implicit, how sure are you that the "expector" really feels the way you think he or she does?
- Does the "expector" have the right to expect this of you at this time?
- Given the appropriate context, would the "expector" understand why you made your choice?
- Could you enact a creative compromise?
- Do you need to forgive yourself?

Dealing with Guilt

Show me a woman who doesn't feel guilty and I'll show you a man.
Erica Jong

About two years ago I received this e-mail the day before Bring Your Daughter to Work Day:

I am bringing my 8-year old daughter to the office tomorrow. Would you have some time around noon to meet with her? I would love her to spend some time with a woman executive. You are a great role model.

I looked at my calendar for that time and saw that I had planned to take the lunch hour to buy furniture for my home office. Guilt quickly descended on me. In truth, I did not want to meet this woman's daughter. I had put off buying a desk for my office far too long; I wanted to go shopping. But there I was, a "role model." How could I say no? The guilt was too much for me, so I asked my assistant to schedule the meeting. Then I immediately told her not to schedule it. She realized something was amiss, so I told her the story. She wisely pulled out a handout on guilt from a Balanced Life seminar and asked just two questions:

Whose expectations was I not meeting? I certainly wouldn't be meeting the expectations of the woman who sent me the e-mail. Neither was I meeting my own expectations that I should help other women in business.

Did the "expector" have the right to expect this of me at this time? Actually, the answer was no. I had never met the woman who sent the e-mail. She was asking for time on very short notice. My company had set up an entire program for the children who were coming that day. Her daughter would have the chance to meet other role models. As for my own expectations, I had already said "No" to participating in the program that year; I had other Personal Priorities.

So I was able to hold back the guilt, politely decline, and went shopping the next day. The fact that I still remember the incident tells you I am not totally guilt free about it and dread the day a woman comes up to me and tells me she is the one who sent the e-mail. But I was able to control the guilt rather than have it control me, which is an important step. I hope you can do the same.

Winning Isn't Everything

Any time you try to win everything,
you must be willing to lose everything.
Larry Csonka

As a competitive type myself, I think winning is great. But trying to win every race every time is impossible, exhausting, and does not lead you down the path to balance. Rather than striving to compete and conquer at every opportunity, try these two techniques. First, remind yourself you don't have to enter every race. Pick one or two that matter to you and try to win those. Don't contend for every promotion or sales award that's dangled in front of you.

Second, tell yourself the game of balance is like a decathlon, the athletic contest that consists of ten different track and field events. You win a decathlon by doing well in each of those events, but you don't have to hold the world's record in any one area. Similarly, if you want balance in your life you need to do well at your job *and* all your other Personal Priorities. Maybe people who care about nothing but their jobs will outperform you. That's all right. You are not striving for the gold medal in work-related performance; you're striving to live the life you want.

By gaining the perspective to appreciate *everything* she was doing, this part-time worker realized she was winning the competition she wanted to be in:

I was feeling bad about working part time when I saw how slowly my career was progressing. I looked at my co-workers getting promoted and felt like I was losing some race. Then I remembered my other priorities, namely my relationship with my partner and my children. Now when I see someone doing better than me careerwise, I compare his or her entire life to my entire life. I realize what a wonderful family I have and what a good job I have, even if it is part time. Whenever I look at life in this way, I always see myself as the winner.

Let Go of Your Urge for Power

We have, I fear, confused power with greatness.
Stewart Udall

Letting loose of the craving for power and control is another challenge faced by those who want balance. To do this, you need to remember how much your Personal Priorities matter to you. Then ask yourself, which would you rather control, what goes on in your work or what goes on in your life? If you spend too much energy seeking power from your work, the power to shape the rest of your life will ebb away. That may be what you'll decide is right for you. On the other hand, maybe you'll make the choice this administrator did:

I (gasp) turned down taking on even more responsibility in my new role despite the fact that I risked having others think, "She can't handle all that." I knew it was the right thing for me and for my other responsibilities to just say no.

The urge to excel at your job—whether it is for the power, the prizes, the praise, or the money—can also be described as ambition. Is ambition a bad thing? No, but it certainly can interfere with your home life. The next chapter will give you a better sense of how ambition affects the choices you make, and how you can manage your ambition to have a more balanced life.

Exploration Exercises

Looking in the Mirror

As you start to create a more balanced life, old habits and patterns will become surprisingly hard to resist. By understanding what motivates your behavior, you will have a better chance of creating change in your life. This exercise will help you recognize some of the motivational forces shaping your life right now.

- Think about some task at work that you were very eager to work on. What motivators were encouraging you?
- Think about some task at work that you have been avoiding or resisting. Why haven't you been motivated to work on that task?
- In the past year or two, have you made a significant lifestyle change for the better (started exercising, changed to a more careful diet, became more responsible about money management, taken up a new hobby)? What motivated you to make the change and what has motivated you to stick with it?
- What motivators will help you to create a more balanced life for yourself?

Commute Questions

(These questions are for you to ponder when you are commuting, waiting in line, etc. Think of them as directed daydreams.)

On your way into work, think about a task that you don't particularly want to do that day. What would motivate you to feel more enthusiastic about that task? Is there anything that you could do that would create some motivation to get you to do the task?

On your way home, think about when your motivation might have flagged during the day. Why did that happen? If you pushed through your lack of enthusiasm, what motivated you? In the future, will you be able to draw on that same motivation when you need it?

Action Step

Have you found it difficult to devote time to one or more of your Personal Priorities? If so, review what motivates you and design a program for yourself that will initiate some activity around that priority. For example, look at this chart:

PERSONAL PRIORITY	WHAT MOTIVATES YOU	POSSIBLE APPROACH
Be physically active	Competition	Make a bet with a friend that by month-end, you can outlast him on the treadmill. (Don't use this approach if you have a heart condition!)
	Money	Put $1 to $5 in a fund every time you exercise and then use that money to buy something special.
	Meeting your own expectations	Measure your degree of physical fitness today and then set realistic goals on where you can be in a month. Write them down and track your progress with them.
Simplify my life	The need for approval	Decide what you can do in the next two weeks to simplify your life. Tell two friends what you are going to do and ask them to join you for coffee or lunch in two weeks to celebrate.
	Peer pressure	Find a friend or acquaintance who also wants a simpler life and form a support group. Share progress and encouragement weekly.
	The need for control	Make a list of how the complexity in one aspect of your life is interfering with your goals. Then determine how having a simpler life will help reestablish your control.

To me, having a balanced life means being in control of decisions related to how I spend my time. This means knowing why I am doing something and being truly OK with it.

A 34-year-old finance director and part-time home remodeler

4

Are You Too Ambitious to Have a Balanced Life?

SEARCHING FOR KEYS

One evening I'm walking past a man on a street corner. He's bending down, looking for something that he seems to have dropped under the streetlight. I ask if I can help him search. He tells me he has dropped his keys.

After looking for several minutes with no luck, I ask if he is sure he has lost them there. "Oh no," he replies. "I dropped them on another corner. But the light is much better here."

Are you sure you are searching in the right spot for the keys to your happiness? Might your keys be on a corner that is less well traveled and not so brightly lit?

Is it possible to be ambitious and have a balanced life? Can you value—in fact, strive for—career success while maintaining a rewarding home life?

To many people, ambition has a bad reputation. "There are no persons capable of stooping so low as those who desire to rise in the world," sneered the Countess of Blessington in 1839, and to many her words ring true today. Yet ambition inspires magnificent achievements. Great presidents, great writers, and great doctors become what they are because somewhere inside they are motivated to do better and achieve more. Does this make them bad people, "capable of stooping low," in the countess's words? Not necessarily, for it is possible to be ambitious and be true to your authentic self. But you have to be conscious and disciplined about the choices you make.

Making Your Choices

It is a strange desire to seek power and to lose liberty.
Francis Bacon

Ambitious men and women who value their home lives constantly struggle with issues of balance. We want it all—business success and personal success. But each day presents us with choices that have to be made—do I stay late for that meeting or watch my daughter's school play? Do I work through lunch or make time to see a friend? Do I have a beer with my boss or go to my softball game? These daily choices represent daily opportunities to set priorities. And when you value career success, it's tempting to *always* choose the work-related activity over the personal activity.

An example of these choices is suggested by the following classified ad:

NEED A BUILDER for my 12 yr old's 13-ft plywood runabout. Frames, stem, transom, etc., are done. Business commitments leave me no time to finish her. Looking for someone to complete hull & deck, ready for paint & rigging. Time is of the essence. Fair price paid. Please help me not disappoint my son.

I contacted the man who ran this ad and this is what he told me:

I have a new job that requires lots of travel so I can't finish building the runabout myself. It's a shame, really. Shipbuilding has been my hobby since I was a teenager. And I want to be able to spend time with my son. It means a lot to both of us. But this new job is important for my career. I had to make a choice and I chose the bigger job. I'll have to find someone else to finish the runabout.

This man believed this boost to his career was more important than wrapping up the building project with his son. Most people who aspire to higher positions would make a similar decision. Yet the last line in the father's ad, "Please help me not disappoint my son," is a poignant reminder of the misgivings the ambitious feel as they make their choices.

The juggling of career ambitions with a home life involves dozens of disquieting decisions. Frequently, knowledge of our Personal Priorities is of little value in these situations because for the ambitious, success at work *is* truly important. It might be expressed as "Getting to the top" or "Achieving goals" or "Being satisfied with my career" or even "Believing my work counts." These all translate into a striving to achieve more, to do great work, or to master the field we've chosen. For the ambitious, having a successful work life is vital. Consistently electing our home lives over the possibility of career advancement is not an option. So how then do we make choices on how to spend our time, especially when both our bosses and our families want us to be with *them*?

Ambitious people who want balance soon learn that they

can't make everybody happy, as ruefully described by this professional woman:

> *"I hate your job!" are the exact words that came out of my 10-year-old daughter's mouth just the other day. When I have an early appointment, the kids have to go to summer camp early. I told her that sometimes I hate the hours of my job, but I like my job—and there were just some days when she'd have to get up and get it together early—like I do for her for her Saturday morning soccer games. Well, she heard me, but she said she still hates my job.*

Trade-offs vs. Sacrifices

What does it profit a man to gain the whole world and forfeit his life?
Mark 8:34

Having balance while still fulfilling career ambitions requires an endless stream of compromises and trade-offs. I'd like to dispel the notion, however, that people make "sacrifices" to balance their business and their home lives. The term *sacrifice* is an emotionally laden exaggeration of the process that takes place. Sacrifice implies placing an offering on an altar with the hope that the gods of the universe will favor the donor sometime in the future. If good fortune comes, it was a fair bargain. But if the gods ignore the gift, then the hopeful beneficiary has set herself up for disappointment. You can almost hear her complaining, "After all I have done, this is how you repay me?"

Rather than sacrifice, I prefer the term *trade-off*. If you are ambitious, you are willing to trade certain components in your life for success. By thinking in terms of trade-offs, you create the paradigm of informed choices that can be negotiated. You are taking your resources to a marketplace and making a series of exchanges.

What can you exchange for the possibility of career success? Generally, trade-offs are made within one of four categories: time, relationships, where you live and work, and your core values and principles.

Time   Time is the most common exchange medium in the quest for success. Unless they have to pay for overtime, most employers have no compunction about asking people to devote more and more time to the workplace. Many Americans now work 45, 50, or even 60 hours a week, significantly higher than the "standard" 40 hours. So instead of happily spending hours in the garden, at the movies, sailing, shopping, or sleeping, we tend to be at work hoping to advance our careers.

Once in the pattern of working long hours, we tend to forget we are making a trade-off. This office worker seems to question if the long hours were worth the price:

> I've worked an average 10-hour day for almost ten years at my company. I have been very successful, yet I'm not fulfilled. That tells me that if I envision a different opus (and I do), I better get started on it!

Relationships   Relationships are another frequently exchanged commodity in the career marketplace. Your professional life cuts into the time available for relationships and also into the emotional energy that's required. The consequences can be seen in relationships that grow apart, relationships that don't advance, and potential friendships that are never created, as this advertising manager found out:

I worked for a marketing firm that hired young, enthusiastic, intelligent people and worked them to the bone. If you left at 5:30 people would tap their watch and say, "Well, aren't you leaving early." The workload was so overwhelming that I left each day with my stress level through the roof. It took a big toll on my relationship with my husband and friends because I had no free time.

<u>Where You Live and Work</u>   Where you work, where you live, and how much you travel can be categorized under geographic trade-offs. The decisions you make here include what city you choose for your home. ("I loved living in Charlotte, but the real opportunities are in New York City.") The length of your commute is also a geographic decision. You may decide that a more interesting job is well worth the two-hour drive on a grid-locked freeway. Another variation is how much you travel—how often do you spend the night away from your own bed?

This woman discovered that she needed more than just a promising career path to keep her happy:

I used to work in consulting and traveled from Sunday evening through Friday evening. I couldn't handle it anymore and so when I went to look for a new job it was to find anything, really anything, which would keep me at home and off the plane.

<u>Core Values</u>   While no one likes to admit it, many of us trade off some part of our core value system to protect or enhance our career success. These value trade-offs are always more obvious in other people's behavior than in our own. But value conflicts we encounter on the job aren't necessarily easy to avoid and are as apt to happen to us as the next person:

I was working as a junior analyst in investment banking. Virtually all of the emotional energy in the place was around generating fees—big ones. And because one can make numbers tell any story, I was often strongly encouraged to "tweak" my assumptions and the numbers for the benefit of the firm. I must admit that, being 21 years old, I had a hard time navigating this.

Time, relationships, where you live and work, and values are not currencies reserved exclusively for the highly ambitious. Subtly or directly, anyone employed in the modern workplace is asked to make trade-offs in each of these categories. Most of the time, the trade-offs are innocuous, like missing a friend's birthday dinner because you're away on a business trip. Other times the trade-offs are significant, like when you are asked to accept a promotion in another state. How many and what kinds of trade-offs you make depends on the level of priority you give to your career and as importantly, how resourceful you are at reaching creative compromises.

The Art of the Creative Compromise

Life is not the way it's supposed to be. It's the way it is. The way you cope with it is what makes the difference.
Virginia Satir

Does wanting a successful, high-powered career and a satisfying home life mean you are asking for too much? It does if you long for limitless career possibilities and a picture-perfect home life. Unquestionably, you have to make trade-offs. But in addition to the willingness to make trade-offs there are some other prerequisites you must fulfill to have career success and balance.

First, you have to have a natural proclivity and passion for your chosen field of endeavor. If you struggle to keep up with your work and to do as well as your peers, it's nearly impossible to further your career and still have energy left for your home life.

The second requirement is to know how to invent solutions to seemingly irresolvable problems. Finding room for a career and a home life is like confronting a 1,000-piece jigsaw puzzle without the benefit of the picture on the box. With few role models and precedents, you have to combine the career pieces and the home pieces of your life and come up with an appealing, interlocking, and sustainable whole. You need to become expert at creative problem solving, coming to win-win solutions, and compromise.

For example, listen to the words of a very successful entrepreneur, who became president of a multimillion dollar communications company by the time he was 40. He made many trade-offs, but he established limits on what he would give to his career and stuck with them. It helped that he was very talented.

My weekends are sacred. I may—and do—travel all over the country during the week, but I am always home on Friday night and stay through Sunday night. That gives me time with my kids and wife and makes me a part of the family again.

What do I trade off by devoting Saturday and Sunday to my family? In my business, a lot of work gets done on the golf course on weekends so I lose out on that. Another trade-off is that I have no friends. I work like a dog all week and weekends are for my family, so that doesn't leave any time to develop friendships. It's too bad, but you just can't have everything.

Here is another example of a creative compromise a working mother made to have career success and a balanced life:

I live in Phoenix and had a four-day business trip to San Francisco. At the same time, my son had won his local Little League game and was going to play in the statewide tournament. Of course, the game was when I going to be away. I had missed another championship game of his a few years ago while traveling on business. At that time, I told myself that I would never let that happen again.

So I flew to San Francisco as scheduled, but the next evening, I flew out again at 5. I got to the game a half hour late and they were behind 7–0. But by the end they rallied and won. Needless to say, my son was ecstatic to have me there. I took a plane out very early the next morning and was able to rejoin my meetings.

This is a good example of making a conscious and creative trade-off. To be able to go on the business trip and see the baseball game, this manager had to relinquish the price of the plane tickets and the opportunity to build relationships with business colleagues for an evening. She also added the stress of two more plane flights. She gained the opportunity to strengthen the relationship with her son and to be true to her values. Of course, we don't know if her long-term career success was harmed by her absence that evening. Nor do we know if her relationship with her son would have been impaired if she had missed the game. We do know, however, that she is very proud of the choice she made.

At other times, the conflicts don't involve family life but staying true to your core values. This computer programmer tells of when he was asked to compromise his principles and what he did instead:

> While in my first programming position at a six-person consulting company, one of the clients was working on temperature-measurement technology and one of its applications was for the military. I'd been a conscientious objector to the Vietnam War, so producing something that would help the military kill people went directly against my core values. I agreed to work on software for the technology—but asked not to work on any direct military customizations. My request was respected.

The next time you are asked to trade off something that matters to you for the sake of your career, realize that you have three choices. You can choose the path that favors your job, the path that favors your home life, or you can blaze a new trail. Sometimes this third option isn't as hard as it may seem. Have faith that a creative compromise is out there somewhere; if you keep looking, you'll find it.

Extracting Yourself from Poor Trade-offs

The trouble with the rat race is that even if you win,
you're still a rat.
Lily Tomlin

If you happen to make a poor choice when you are trying to balance your home and your work life, you'll appreciate another benefit of using the "trade-off" paradigm instead of a "sacrifice" paradigm. By recognizing your choices as trades, you realize you can renegotiate some of the deals you have made in the past. Perhaps there are some decisions you have made that you want to reconsider. For example, think about how happy you are with your geographic choices. Do you live where you want to? Are you traveling too much? Is your commute too long? What did you accomplish by making those trade-offs? Has it been worth it? If not, maybe it's time to make another trade.

Listen to the story of this systems analyst:

I worked at a small consulting firm whose headquarters were near my home. Unfortunately, the client I was assigned to was 40 miles further south on a very crowded freeway. Overall, my commute took three hours out of my day. I listened to a lot of books on tape and really liked my job, so I thought I was handling it just fine.

It took my wife to get me to see what the commute was doing to my life. She made it clear that she missed me and felt I wasn't spending enough time with the kids. So even though I really was really happy with my job and the people, I started looking around. I found two jobs I liked and now my commute is just forty-five minutes by train.

Sometimes you take a job full of high hopes only to find that your new environment asks you to make trade-offs you are uncomfortable with. If the requests are particularly egregious, you may chose to walk out, no matter how it might look on your résumé. When this account supervisor found herself in an untenable situation, she realized she had to quit:

I worked at an ad agency that would do or say anything—outright lies—to get new business. They cared nothing about doing a good job once we got the client. It was disgusting and frustrating. I lasted only seven months. It really shocked me that these supposed "reputable" businesspeople could be so sleazy.

Changing jobs, or even changing careers, are steps taken by thousands of individuals striving for more balance in their lives. The trend toward downshifting, or taking a less challenging career in order to create a better lifestyle, is a prime example of people renegotiating the trade-offs they made in the past. No longer satisfied with their executive positions or high-pressured professions, individuals are starting new careers as teachers, counselors, and even ministers. Have they lost their ambition? Maybe, or maybe they are choosing to play a different game. Needless to say, for the ambitious, this is not a decision that comes easily.

This financial manager was surprised to find that his desire to maintain a certain way of life outweighed his ambition:

I was asked to take a broader role in a different city and I declined due to quality of life issues. It was the first time I had ever made that kind of decision. I suspect that in the future, my way of allowing more time for priorities may involve "plateauing" my level of responsibilities and performance. This will be very difficult for me to do. Overcoming fears of professional "failure" (getting off the "type A train") will be tough.

Is It Possible to Avoid Bad Trade-offs?

When folk tell me of this great man and that great man, I think to myself, Who was stinted of joy for his glory?
Mary Webb

While it's generally possible to renegotiate poor trade-offs, it's preferable to avoid them in the first place. Some choices have more dire consequences than others do. Most of us can cite friends or work associates who suffer from divorce, estrangement from their children, or poor health because they work too many hours. There is rarely a single decision that leads to these tragedies; instead, the heartache arises from a long sequence of poor trade-offs. The consequences of overwork are insidious. Inexorably and surreptitiously, a workaholic's habits erode her health and home life, until the damage is too deep to disregard and her world begins to deteriorate about her.

Bad trade-offs for the sake of a career come in many different forms, but they frequently involve relationships. Creating a solid relationship with another human being is in itself a challenge. It becomes even more complex as we try to foster relationships while maximizing our chances for career success. A major drawback is that we frequently have imperfect information. Your spouse may say it's all right to take a more demanding job assignment but not really mean it. Or she may not like the consequences once the decision's made, yet you don't want to go back to the bargaining table. Sometimes circumstances change after we make our decisions. A child may suddenly demonstrate developmental needs just as you agree to take on significantly more responsibility. Do you change the deal with your boss? Another example of the cost of incomplete information is the woman who puts off pregnancy "for a few years" while she advances her career. Later she finds she has fertility problems due to her age. Since she can't go back in time to make a different trade-off, she has to deal with the situation that faces her today.

An ambitious executive tells her story:

> I knew that I really wanted to become the chief financial officer of the firm I'm working for. I was very good at my job and was confident I could manage the top spot. But I didn't want to be pregnant or to have a baby while I was trying to get promoted or learning a new job, so we put off having a family for several years. It never occurred to me that I wouldn't eventually have a child. Now we are trying and it's not so easy. I'm undergoing fertility treatments, but nothing has worked so far. Every month I'm on an emotional roller coaster. But if I had to do it all over again, I still think I would make the same decision. Of course, I can say that today because I still believe we're going to have a baby.

Unfortunately, as this story illustrates, if you're an ambitious woman who also wants to start a family, there's no way to know what the end results of your trade-off will be. No one can predict with any certainty how hard it might be for a particular woman to get pregnant, whether she is trying next month or in ten years' time. Sometimes, women ask me whether it's better to have babies while they are still relatively young or to first establish themselves in the work world. I can't answer that question for them and neither can anyone else. What any particular woman should do depends greatly on what she wants and how badly she would miss developing the alternative. I remember myself as a newlywed, clad in my

1980s dress-for-success suit and sobbing in my husband's arms because I was afraid I was pregnant. I had just started a new job and I didn't want any baby to interfere with the next rung on my career ladder. It turned out to be a false alarm. My first child was born three years later, after I had time to let my ambition run unencumbered for a while.

While some unfortunate choices are made because all the important facts aren't available, at other times people make bad trade-offs because they don't want to deal with the consequences of better information. It is easier, and more exciting, to grab for the brass ring of career success and hope the repercussions are bearable. We ask for forgiveness rather than permission. Or sometimes we know our career-favoring decision will cause problems at home, but in truth we would rather succeed on the job than in a particular relationship. Consider the words of a hard-driving professional:

> There were many times when I was married to Cheryl that I worked long hours just because it was more rewarding, and frankly, lots more pleasant to be at the office than at home arguing with her. It's no surprise that we eventually divorced. That marriage wasn't successful, but I like to think my career benefited from those extra hours.

Accepting Uncertainty

What's the use of running if you're on the wrong road?
Anonymous

There are no surefire prescriptions for making perfect trade-offs for career success. You can conscientiously gather the best information available and still make mistakes. But if you are making trade-offs about relationships, don't try to fool yourself or others. Be as honest and as communicative as you can. Encourage those you care about to do the same.

Even when you do all that, until you have lived through a situation it is hard to know the true price of trade-offs you made. When I decided to work on this book, I took a leave of absence from my job, partially to have the time to write but also to spend more time with my family. As I was finishing up my writing, my boss offered me a new job, one with lots of responsibilities and quite a bit of travel. Suddenly I had to ask myself what trade-offs I was willing to make. I could choose to stay away from the corporate life and have a more relaxed schedule as a writer and speaker. Or I could propel myself back into the demanding world I had left behind. My ambition ruled and I took the corporate job, figuring I could make enough creative compromises to keep balance in my life. But on my first business trip, when I was going to be away for over a week, my 8-year-old daughter lashed out at me. "Why do you have to go? I don't want you to go. You told me you quit and now you're working again," she cried. As I heard my soothing words to her, another part of my mind was asking, "Have I already made a bad trade?" I sincerely hope not.

Having ambitions for a career makes it harder to have a balanced life, but it's not impossible. Ambition is only bad when we are willing to make too many trade-offs. For while ambition itself is not blind, it can blind us. At that point, even if we don't realize it, our actions tell the world our tragic secret, that nothing is more important to us than success on the job.

Exploration Exercises

Looking in the Mirror
Take some time to contemplate and complete the worksheet here. The first column helps you reflect on the trade-offs that you have made in the past, whether they were good or bad. The second column gives you a chance to reconsider some of these trade-offs and whether you might want to change them. The third column provides you with the opportunity to set limits on your ambition so you won't trade away one set of priorities for the appeal of another. Start with the column that appeals to you the most.

Ambitions Trade-offs Worksheet

	What trade-offs have you made in the past in order to further your career?	How (if at all) would you like to adjust the trade-offs you have made?	What would you not trade off, no matter how appealing the job opportunity?
MY TIME			
MY RELATIONSHIPS			
WHERE I LIVE AND WORK			
ADHERING TO MY CORE VALUES			

Commute Questions
(These questions are for you to ponder when you are commuting, waiting in line, etc. Think of them as directed daydreams.)

- Do you have a particularly onerous commute? If so, did you end up there as a result of your desire to advance your career? Were you aware of the implications of the trade-off you made? Are you still satisfied with the trade-off, or do you need to make a change?
- Is your commute a pleasant one? How important is a pleasant commute to your satisfaction with your life? Would you trade off your current commute for a more appealing job but a less appealing commute?

Action Steps

1. Refer back to the Ambition Trade-offs Worksheet, particularly the column on what trade-offs you might want to adjust. Create a plan on how you might renegotiate those trades during the next year.
2. If you have a spouse or partner, share some or all of your Ambition Trade-offs Worksheet with him or her. Since relationship trade-offs are often plagued with imperfect information, use this opportunity to share your thoughts with the loved one who would be most affected by any trade-offs you decide to make. Does your partner see your trade-offs differently than you do? Does he or she think you've made trade-offs that you haven't listed or acknowledged? If you haven't done so already, this would also be an excellent time to share your Personal Priorities with your partner in order to give him or her a context for the decisions you are making.

> To me, having a balanced life means loving my life, whatever I am doing. I don't believe that you have to stop and smell the roses to have a balanced life ... as long as you are carrying (and cherishing) the roses with you.
>
> An author, Ph.D., and management consultant

Part 2:

RECLAIMING YOUR TIME

It will never rain roses: when we want

To have more roses we must plant more trees.

George Eliot

Where to Find the Time You Need

THE OVERLOOKED GIFT

From the heights of heaven, a god and goddess look down on a villager. "Look at that poor man," says the goddess. "He is pure of heart yet suffers so. His crops have died, his children are sick, and he has no money for food or medicine. If no help comes to him soon, they will all die. Please, give him a bag of gold to relieve him of his burdens."

"He will not use it," answers the god, "so I don't want to give it to him."

But the goddess keeps insisting, so the god finally drops a bag of gold in the pathway of the poor villager. The man barely glances at the bag as he hurries past.

What gifts lie in your path that you do not take the time to discover?

It is time to talk about how you use your time. Finding more time in your day makes creating a balanced life easier. The more discretionary time you have, the fewer difficult trade-offs you have to make and the less stressed you feel.

But finding more time is always a challenge. We have all tried a plethora of time management techniques and still believe that we haven't enough time. And at some level, that belief is true. There is not enough time for everything. But there is enough time for the important things. The universe grants each of us 24 hours each day, 168 hours each week, 8,760 hours each year. If we are conscious how we use those hours, if we allocate our time wisely among those things that are important to us, there is enough time. Barely. But there's no time to squander foolishly.

As important as it is to find more time in your day, it's only of secondary importance when it comes to creating a balanced life. The more critical task is to allocate your hours to what is important. Therefore, time management for a balanced life requires some special approaches. These three guiding principles can help:

1. Make the best use of the time you have.
2. Leave work at a specified departure hour.
3. Say "No" to requests not related to your Personal Priorities.

A time management approach that does *not* work is attempting to do more and more in less and less time. I used to think that if I could master doing three things at once I could actually accomplish everything I needed to do. I remember trying to paint my fingernails while riding my stationary bike while reading the newspaper. My polish smeared, I never got any exercise because I kept stopping to redo my nails, and after ten minutes I still hadn't made it through the front page. In truth, this type of multiphasic behavior is not only inefficient, it also leads to increased stress. Your objective should not be how to do more simultaneously, but how to do less and do it well.

Always remember that time is the most precious gift you possess. Money and material belongings can always be replaced, but once an hour flows past, it is gone forever. As you try to create more balance in your life, never forget that time is your dearest resource. Uncover more hours for yourself and use them in a way that best serves your soul.

The First Principle: Make the Best Use of the Time You Have

In truth, people can generally make time for what they choose to do:
it is not really the time but the will that is lacking.
Sir John Lubbock

Since time is so valuable, we can't afford to be careless with it. Yet sometimes, unthinkingly, we get distracted and spend our time poorly. What is a poor use of time? Any period of time, even as little as ten minutes, that we spend on something that is neither a Personal Priority nor some truly necessary chore. This doesn't mean every moment has to be "productive." On the contrary, if "Appreciating the beauty around me" is on your Personal Priority list, a good use of time might be watching a butterfly sun herself on a leaf. But in order to have the time to watch the butterfly *and* enjoy a fulfilling career, you have to be conscious of how you spend the hours you have.

We all indulge in time-wasters that don't contribute to the development of our Personal Priorities. Think about what you do during the day—what habits have you developed that fritter away your priceless time? After working on her Personal Priorities, this woman became more aware of when she was spending her time poorly:

Knowing my Personal Priorities has made me aware of "little"
time-wasters—like watching a TV show simply because it

comes on before or after something I really want to watch. (Watching bad TV shows wasn't part of any of my Priorities.) Now, I am much more conscious about spending my time on what's important to me.

Another way to spend time wisely is to spend less time on all those ostensibly necessary chores. The six techniques described next—prioritizing, delegating, simplifying, setting time limits, procrastinating, and eliminating—let you accomplish what needs to be done in less time than you might imagine. They work equally well in your home life and your work life. Whenever I'm feeling confounded by too much to do, I know I'm not letting these techniques protect me from my own compulsions.

Time-Saver 1: Prioritize

We say we waste time, but that is impossible. We waste ourselves.
Alice Block

Prioritizing means that you take what is most important and stick it at the top of your to-do list, bumping everything else one level down if not off the list completely. Then, and this is the hard part, discipline yourself to dedicate your time to completing what's on the top of the list.

This leasing agent tells how she remains true to her work priorities:

Because of my child-care situation, I work fewer hours than the other partners in my office so I focus on being extremely efficient. For example, I never socialize at work. Once we hired a friend of mine as a contractor and during her first morning she came into my office with her cup of coffee to sit down and chitchat. It was kind of awkward, but I had to tell her to leave. When I'm at work, I don't have time to chat.

Effective prioritizing requires that you let lots of activities languish, no matter how pleasant or how obligatory they seem. When you're working on a task that has the highest priority, everything else has to wait.

When I asked a single mom how she managed to get everything done, this is the answer she gave me:

Living things come first. When I get home from work and the house is a mess and the groceries need to be put away and my daughter is hungry, I remind myself that living things come first. So I ignore the messy kitchen, let the groceries sit on the counter, and make sure my daughter gets her snack. And I find as I watch her sweet face get smeared with jam, I am truly content. The mess and the groceries don't matter. What matters is how much I love my daughter.

Time-Saver 2: Delegate

Ask and it shall be given you.
Matthew 7:7

Whether you consider a task important or unimportant, you should always ask yourself, who else could be doing this work?

A colleague, a secretary, your boss, a supplier, a spouse, a child? Whether you are a manager or a parent, learning to delegate important work while ensuring it will be done well is one of the most valuable skills you can develop.

A colleague who is responsible for both a field sales force and a headquarters support group told me of his technique:

> Whenever I manage people, I always try to give away as much responsibility as possible to those who work for me. And I try very hard to be accepting of the choices they make, even if I might have approached things differently. Everybody seems to win from this approach. The people that work for me like it because they get lots of responsibility with minimal interference. The company benefits because a whole new level of management is being trained to act independently. And of course, I consider myself the big winner because I have time to do other things.

Take a critical look at the managers in your company. Is there a pattern where managers who are the poorest delegators work the longest hours? Which type of manager do you want as your role model?

Delegation techniques can also work at home, as this real estate broker discovered:

> I find if I plan simple meals for each night of the week, I save time grocery shopping, and I can delegate the preparation to my husband. The meals are easy for him to fix and all the ingredients are there.

It is not immoral to ask for help, nor is it risky to entrust responsibility to the right person. Once you get in the habit of delegating, you'll find it's a most satisfying way to reclaim an hour for your own Priorities.

Time-Saver 3: Simplify

Our life is frittered away by detail. Simplify, simplify.
Henry David Thoreau

Making a task simpler can frequently salvage time. Ask yourself what is the purpose of the task you are doing. Strip it down to its essence. Then deliver that and no more. Adding unnecessary bells and whistles to straightforward jobs can waste an amazing amount of time. A good way to check for unnecessary additions is to ask yourself, "Does anyone but me care about this?" If the answer is no, stop doing it.

My best lesson in simplification came when I was complaining to a friend about the need to bake a batch of cupcakes for a school picnic.

"You do use canned frosting, don't you?" she asked. Since I consider myself a good cook, I was appalled and hotly denied using any such conveniences.

"Why not?" she countered. "Are you going to eat the cupcakes? Is any grown-up going to eat the cupcakes? Do the kids care what kind of frosting is on them?"

As I was recognizing the power of her logic, she added, "It's OK to use canned frosting. My therapist said so."

Time-Saver 4: Set Time Limits

Work expands so as to fill the time available for its completion.
Northcote C. Parkinson

Make it clear to yourself and others that there is only so much time you will spend on a particular task. This is a particularly effective technique if you find that people are frequently asking for your help or to discuss something with you. By setting a limit, for example, explaining up front that you have only ten minutes you can spare, you encourage those around you to focus on the problem at hand. Plus you can then end the conversation after ten minutes and not feel guilty.

This purchasing agent found that setting time limits really worked for him:

Communicating to co-workers that "I only have 10 minutes" is exceptionally helpful. I accomplish much more during the 8 to 5 time period and feel less obligated to hang out here all evening. It also makes me more aware of other people's time. Whenever I think of stopping at someone's desk to run something by them, I ask myself how I would feel if someone just popped in and asked me something like this. Usually, I try to find some other way of taking care of the situation.

Time-Saver 5: Procrastinate

We all procrastinate at one time or another. The most unfortunate
procrastination of all is to put off being happy.
Maureen Mueller

While procrastination, or deferring a task to some unspecified time, has a poor moral connotation, it is a very effective time-saver for unimportant work. You keep postponing a low-priority task until it is no longer necessary or until someone cares enough to make it important for you.

This man tells how he used procrastination (carefully) to his advantage:

> *During one period of my career I put off writing monthly sta-*
> *tus reports for three years before my boss even noticed! If he*
> *had asked, I would have started doing them. But since he didn't*
> *ask, how important could they be? Then I got a new boss and*
> *he noticed the absence immediately. So I was back to writing*
> *status reports, but at least I had enjoyed a three-year reprieve.*

Another procrastination example comes from this over-worked office manager:

> *Sometimes I'll have fifteen telephone messages I am supposed*
> *to return at the end of the day. I'll call back the most impor-*
> *tant ones, but the others I will just set aside. If the person cares*
> *enough to call back, then I'll return the call. But lots of times,*
> *whoever is calling has already gotten an answer somewhere else*
> *and I have kept my workload under control, somewhat.*

Time-Saver 6: Eliminate

Besides the noble art of getting things done, there is the noble art
of leaving things undone. The wisdom of life consists in the
elimination of nonessentials.
Lin Yutang

Eliminating is the most efficient time-saver there is. Take all of the relatively unimportant stuff on your to-do list and decide not to do it. If you feel guilty about it, go back over the section on guilt on pages 43–47. Discipline yourself not to do tasks that don't need to be done, and your payback will be a more balanced life.

Nearly anyone who works in an office can quickly eliminate work by taking a critical look at your "to-read" pile. Can you guess the date of the bottom article in the stack? Is it even from this millennium? Obviously, if that reading were important you would have done it already. Practice your timesaving techniques and throw the whole stack away, as this contractor did:

> It is been a great benefit to be able to come to grips with my "Things to Read" folder. I now get "real" and toss things I won't ever find the time to read. It is a very freeing experience.

Mothers of young children find that by relaxing certain societal standards, they can eliminate many of the chores associated with child rearing.

> I don't tell this to everyone, but I've given up on making my daughter take a bath every day. There just isn't enough time

and a good hand and face washing does almost as good a job. Plus, many nights she sleeps in her next-day clothes. That saves the hassle of getting her in and out of her pj's.

Saving time through the techniques of prioritizing, delegating, simplifying, setting time limits, procrastinating, and eliminating will free up hours in your week. Now how will you spend those newfound hours? Will you do more office work, or will you devote that found time to your other Personal Priorities? To make sure your other Personal Priorities get the time they require, you need to follow the second principle: Leave at your departure hour.

The Second Principle: Leave at Your Departure Hour

God respects me when I work, but he loves me when I sing.
Rabindranath Tagore

What is a "departure hour"? Colloquially it is known as "quitting time," but that phrase has bad connotations. Balanced people aren't quitters—they move from one meaningful aspect of their lives to another. Thus your departure hour is the hour you need to leave your work in order to make sure you have time for your other Personal Priorities. People who don't establish a departure hour, who work until the work is "done," are trapped on the workaholic's hamster wheel. We all know the work is never "done"—laboring into the night won't make the wheel stop spinning. It will just prevent you from having a balanced life.

After attending a Balanced Life course, this analyst realized that many of her long hours at work had probably been wasted.

Prior to the class I was the typical person who wouldn't leave until everything was complete and my desk was bare, even if that meant working twelve or fourteen hours a day. Since the class I have realized that after working ten hours my productivity and quality of my work is definitely decreasing. So why stick around for a couple more hours to finish up something that I could probably do in less than an hour the next day?

While working an extra hour or two seems to be a relatively harmless habit, it actually has an extremely negative consequence on your home life. We tend to believe that staying at work for an extra hour just means we will have an hour less at home. While in a literal sense this is true, in a relative sense it is absolutely *not* true! All hours do not have the same value. On a typical weekday, you spend many hours at work and only a few waking hours at home. If you lengthen your workday by an hour or two, you are increasing it by 10% to 12%. On the other hand, you are decreasing the scarce evening hours you spend at home by 30% to 50%. And that really hurts!

I call this concept "the relative value of an extra hour" and in my opinion, it's one of the most potent concepts you can use to build a balanced life. Let me use a personal example to show you the power of this idea. Many nights I would try to squeeze one more hour in at work. And then when I got home, the evenings were just awful. I felt rushed and my family was cranky. Dinner was a blur, getting the kids to bed was nothing but nag, nag, nag, and by the time my head hit the pillow, I was just as wound up as I had been the second I walked in the door.

What happened? Why did staying late at work just one more hour totally destroy my evening? Certainly the extra hour I spent at work wasn't so wonderful that it compensated for the lousy time I spent at home. If I had been thinking about the "relative value of an extra hour," I could have predicted and prevented the whole situation. Here is the reason why.

Let's say that on a typical day I start work at 8 and leave the office at 6 to be home by 7. Bedtime for my children is 9. Under my normal schedule, I have two hours to have dinner with my family, hear about their day, get the children ready for bed, read them stories and tuck them in.

But on the evening I worked an extra hour, I didn't get home until 8. Bedtime was still at 9, so I had only one hour. I hurried through a leftover dinner alone (the family had eaten without me in front of the TV). I raced the kids through their teethbrushing, skipped their story, and dropped them into bed. I was stressed out, my family was resentful, and the evening time together was ruined.

My mistake was my decision to work an extra hour, turning a 10-hour day into an 11-hour day, a 10% increase. By making that decision, I cut my at-home time with my family from two hours down to one. That is a 50% decrease. And the value of that hour I had left was spoiled because it was so rushed.

Appreciating the Value of an Extra Hour

How we spend our days is, of course, how we spend our lives.
Annie Dillard

Once you understand the concept of "the relative value of an extra hour," it will change the way you approach your work-days. Each hour becomes much more precious. This isn't solely because you want to make the best use of time at work; it's also because the hours in your home life are so limited. It becomes clear that a little time saved from your workday can have a tremendously positive impact on your home life.

Here's an example from a supervisor who came to a Balanced Life course:

> *The relative value of an extra hour was incredibly powerful to me. It made me recognize how much I was giving up on the other side. As I organize my day, I try to anticipate if I'll have to stay late. Then I'll either delegate or simplify or even put off some tasks so I can get everything done and prevent having to stay late. It's made me more aware that while I enjoy working hard and doing a good job, that I'm not paid to be at the "beck and call" of my job 24 hours a day.*

Combining the idea of a departure hour with the knowledge of the relative value of an extra hour will transform how you approach the end of your workday. This attorney's e-mail describes how she put these ideas into practice:

> *Overall, I have definitely been more aware of trying to leave "on time" as many days of the week as possible. Leaving on time lets me get chores done during the week and that has had a dramatic effect on my weekends. I can now spend hours doing things I love or spending time with my boyfriend, without a lot of pressure. I don't have as much "stuff to do" lingering. There is a definite positive domino effect to spending more time on myself. I have noticed a tremendous difference in my attitude—much more positive—and my skin is clearer from more regular sleep :)*

Leaving earlier helped this architect with both his work and his home life:

For me, the departure pledge was the biggest help to me. Putting in an hour more on the job will help (sometimes), but taking that hour for exercise or quality family time actually makes me be more efficient at work.

Leaving Work When You're the Boss

Success is important only to the extent that it puts one in a position to do more things one likes to do.
Sarah Caldwell

When you are self-employed the concept of a departure hour can be even harder to institute. This freelance writer tells of her experience:

I pulled an "all-nighter" last night like I used to do in college. I had a deadline, got caught up in my writing, and kept working until dawn. Of course, I'm a zombie today and might be tomorrow, too. But the good thing about being self-employed is that I can sleep late or take a nap if I want to. I feel I have a lot of balance in my life—I just run by my own schedule. Needless to say, I couldn't take this approach if I had kids.

Many self-employed people, particularly those who work at home, find that children help reinforce the idea of a departure hour. This artist tells his story:

I'm up before dawn to do my painting. That way I can get two to three hours in before my girls wake up. After I get them off to school, I go back to my work and keep at it until they come home around 3:30. Sure, I'd love to keep painting even after they're home, but I rarely do my best work then. If I want to create something worthwhile, it has to be done in those early morning hours.

Being self-employed usually means your next paycheck depends solely on your productivity. Under that kind of pressure, it's sometimes hard to pry yourself away from your work. But before you resign yourself to dawn-to-dusk workdays, take a hard look at the effectiveness of your principal employee, namely you. Do you rate a perfect 10 in how you spend each hour? Are you getting into the office as soon as you can in the morning, or by any chance are you lingering over the paper and a second cup of coffee? If you pushed all six timesaving techniques to their maximum effect, could you accomplish the same amount of work in less time?

When you find you're working past your departure hour, remind yourself of the logic you used when you decided to become self-employed. Weren't you happily anticipating having more control over your time? So take advantage of that control. Use whatever timesaving tricks you can to close up the day's projects and go on to your other Priorities. Believe me, those worker bees in big bureaucracies covet your freedom.

Strategies for Leaving at Your Departure Hour

Those that wish to sing always find a song.
Swedish proverb

Having a departure hour reminds you of the need to go home while there are still hours of value waiting for you there. Yet you sometimes have to convince other people, particularly your boss and/or co-workers, that you're serious about leaving at a particular time. A number of strategies are useful in getting out the door. One graduate of a Balanced Life class tells of her experience:

> I get in at 7 and leave by 4:30 or 5 every day, no matter what. This creates time for helping my three children with their homework and gives us time for dinner together. I have often been asked, "Can you be flexible and stay later?" Unless the requested meeting is absolutely critical, I respond, "My day begins at 7 and I have other commitments in the evening." At this point, very few people ask for 5 P.M. meetings anymore.

Some people find such a straightforward approach unworkable in their situations. One man sets his pager to go off at 5:45. He glances at it, mumbles about how he has to go, and dashes out the door. Another woman who attended a Balanced Life class wanted to get home so she could spend more hours with her dog. She believed (and probably rightfully so) her boss would be unsympathetic to her concerns. So I suggested that if asked, she tell her boss that she had to leave because she had a commitment to meet someone who was expecting her at a certain hour. Unfortunately he wasn't accessible by phone or pager so she couldn't be late. While this might be stretching the situation a tad, it was truthful.

Frankly, bosses and co-workers don't have the right to evaluate your reasons for leaving work. Companies do have the right to evaluate the quantity and quality of the work you do. But once you have fulfilled your daily duty, you have no obligation to tell them why you're leaving. So give a reason if you must, but keep it short. Don't give enough information to let anyone second-guess you. This engineer learned how freeing it was once he no longer felt compelled to give excuses:

> *The most useful thing for me was the realization that I don't need to explain everything to people at work. So if I leave "early" at 5:30 P.M. when I've already put in nine hours, I don't need to say, "Well, I've got to meet someone at 6 P.M." I can just leave without explaining. And if someone asks, I just tell them that I've got a prior commitment. I've helped some other people with this concept. It's very liberating!*

Standing up for yourself and your right to a departure hour is one challenge. A similar challenge stalks each of us at work *and* in our home lives. This challenge is how to say "No" to people who want us to do things for them. Like spending time consciously and leaving work at your departure hour, knowing how to say "No" is a guiding principle for creating a balanced life.

The Third Principle: Say "No" to Requests Not Related to Your Priorities

Happy the man, and happy he alone
He, who can call today his own.
John Dryden

In order to have some balance in your life, you have to learn to be discriminating in the responsibilities you take on. Spending your priceless hours wisely requires that you reject certain activities, no matter how worthwhile they may sound. As soon as someone asks you to do something that's a significant time commitment, immediately check the request against your Personal Priorities. Is it something that's important to you? Does this Personal Priority need some time and attention? If yes, then go ahead and commit. If not, politely refuse and don't feel guilty. This marketing consultant gives a good example:

I have started saying no to invitations to go places and do things without my family. The Balanced Life class validated my commitment to make my family a priority, and I know my real friends will understand. People would always say to me, "You have to go out more" or "You stay home all the time on weekends." I started wondering if something was wrong with me. Now I understand that being home is what's important to my children and me right now and that's what I'll do.

How to Say "No" with Comfort

When you take my time, you take something I had meant to use.
Marianne Moore

Many people don't say "No" often enough because they don't know how. An unadorned "No" seems too curt and rude. Yet embellishments seem to obscure the message and perpetuate the discussion until your "No" is somehow twisted into a "Yes." In order to stick with your "No," you have to remember you are turning down one request because you are preserving your time for more important activities, those associated with your Personal Priorities. But you can't say, "No, I will not work on your fund-raising event because it is not a Personal Priority of mine." Therefore, you need a satchel full of catch phrases that constitute polite but firm refusals. To help you remember, I have categorized them by the timesaving techniques of prioritizing, delegating, simplifying, setting time limits, procrastinating, and eliminating.

Six Easy Ways to Say "No"
- *Prioritize.* "I am sorry I can't help with that. I have so many other commitments, I can't add anything more to my plate."
- *Delegate:* "I am sorry I won't be able to help you. Have you asked Ms. X or Mr. Y? They might be able to help."
- *Simplify:* "I can't commit to everything you are asking for, but if there is something simple I can do, let me know."
- *Set Time Limits:* "I am tight on time these days so I could only spend a few minutes on your project."

- *Procrastinate:* "I really can't commit to that now. Maybe some other time."
- *Eliminate:* "I am sorry. I don't have the time to do that kind of activity anymore."

As you start to use these techniques and find your own way to phrase your "No's," you'll be pleasantly surprised by how good it makes you feel. Listen to this entrepreneur's experience:

I have learned to get creative in how to turn others' requests of my time back to them. And I am getting better at telling people that this expectation of me is not reasonable at this time. I appreciate having a diplomatic way to say it. . . . It's really difficult for me to confront someone's expectation head on and basically say no. But it needs to be done, and sometimes the sooner the better.

This executive also found how effective polite refusals could be at her workplace:

I've become expert at saying, "I have another meeting that I really need/want to attend" or "I have a prior commitment that I can't miss." My new philosophy is just say "No," and don't look back. It works better for me, and it works better for the folks around me, since I am not trying to do everything or being "wishy-washy" about participating in things.

You may find that you are using a combination of these responses to preserve your time for yourself. If you do, remember there's a great advantage in not volunteering more information than you absolutely must. Involved explanations give other people levers they can use to try to change your mind.

Plus the conversation itself takes time. So say "No" quickly and politely. Then quietly congratulate yourself for actively choosing a more balanced life.

Exploration Exercises

Looking in the Mirror

1. What are the little activities that you do during the day that don't add much joy or value to your life? On a piece of paper, list those marginal activities. (On my list, there would be things like watching *Frasier* and *Murphy Brown* reruns, wandering around the Internet searching for a trivial tidbit of information, and poring over catalogs when I don't need to buy anything.) Opposite each one, write down an alternative you could do instead that would support one of your Personal Priorities. What is preventing you from substituting a Personal Priority activity for what you were doing before?

2. Write a list of tasks that you dislike doing for either your work life or your home life. If you need some inspiration, go back to the drawing of the scales you made in Chapter 1. Think how you could stop doing at least some of those dreary tasks through the timesaving techniques of prioritizing, delegating, simplifying, setting time limits, procrastinating, and/or eliminating. (Obviously, these techniques can also be applied to tasks we enjoy doing, but generally we are far more motivated to figure out how we can stop doing what we don't like to do!)

Commute Questions

(These questions are for you to ponder when you are commuting, waiting in line, etc. Think of them as directed daydreams.)

- Do you find yourself overcommitted at home or at work? If so, pretend someone's asking for your time and practice saying "No" with the appropriate excuses. (If you commute alone, rehearse your excuses out loud.) Do this so often that saying "No" becomes a habit.

- On your commute home, ask yourself if you agreed to do something earlier in the day that you now regret. Why didn't you say "No"? Learn from this incident so it won't happen to you next time.

Action Step

Review the lists you created in the first part of these exercises. Now think about one of your Personal Priorities that hasn't been getting enough time from you. Decide how you can create time for that Priority, either by eliminating your time-wasters or by delegating, simplifying, or abolishing one of the tasks you don't want to do.

> To me, having a balanced life means never having to worry about having the time to do the things I love and to be with the people I care about.
>
> A 50+-year-old project manager, music lover, and single parent

Two Approaches for Especially Busy Times

THE GRASSHOPPER AND THE ANT: THE SEQUEL

During the glorious autumn days, a grasshopper does nothing but sing his happy song. Meanwhile, the little ants work ceaselessly gathering food for the winter ahead.

When the days grow colder, the grasshopper can find nothing to eat and is slowly starving. The ants take pity on him and invite him into their home. Once there, he is very surprised to see that the previously industrious ants aren't working at all. Instead, they're playing cards, telling stories, and learning new dance steps. Shocked, the grasshopper tells the queen ant that her subjects are slacking off.

"Of course, they don't work now," says the queen. "All autumn we work very hard getting our food, but now is the time for some fun. After all, even an ant deserves joy in his life."

Would your life be happier if you interspersed periods of concentrated work with time spent on more pleasant activities?

By now, you should be well down the path of creating a more balanced life for yourself. You have your list of what is deeply important to you and what you want to spend time on. You understand what motivates you. You can control your feelings of guilt so you don't feel compelled to commit yourself unnecessarily. You can rein in your ambition so it doesn't disrupt your balanced life. In fact, your life is in such perfect balance that you're twisting around to pat yourself on the back.

But now reality returns. You look at next week's schedule and it's worse than ever. You whip through the time-saver list, from prioritizing to eliminating, and you still don't see how you'll finish everything that needs to be done. Forsaking your departure hour looks like the only option. Like it or not, you're stuck spending innumerable hours on your job.

But before you despair of losing your balance completely, let me tell you about two tactics that you can use to maintain your commitment to your Personal Priorities even as your workload swells. These are called pulsing and phasing. *Pulsing* is when you schedule yourself to work long hours a few days a week while still leaving at a reasonable time on other days. *Phasing* is working long hours day after day for extended periods, but knowing when the end date of the work marathon will be.

Pulsing: Some Nights On, Some Nights Off

To keep a lamp burning we have to keep putting oil in it.
Mother Teresa

Pulsing is a great way to demonstrate dedication to your job while preserving time for a rich home life. By scheduling one, two, or perhaps even three days a week to work late (or to come in early), you create time to write memos, catch up on your filing, and touch base with your overworked colleagues. Your "off" nights are still free for your other Personal Priorities. This technique is surprisingly easy to execute, as this accountant testifies:

I leave the office at 5 P.M. twice a week. I tell people, "I have an obligation that requires I leave promptly at 5." No one has questioned this practice at all—I've not even gotten the dirty looks or "why" questions I expected! It's great. And the couple of times someone has asked me to make a late appointment, I let them know that it's not possible on the two days I leave at 5, but the other days are fair game. This seems to work just fine.

Pulsing is an excellent method of fine-tuning the balance you create between hours spent on the job and hours spent at home. Sometimes leaving a job at 5 or 6 every night without fail isn't the best choice for either your home life or your job, as discovered by this working father:

I used to have a strict goal to be home by 6 every night, and I was miserable. On the one hand, I wasn't accomplishing what I wanted at work. On the other, I was frequently late, causing conflict and hurt feelings at home and making the time I was there less valuable as I worried about work and defended my lateness.

Then I changed my schedule so that several nights a week I can be at home on time without fail. The other nights I stay at work as long as I need, until I am caught up. This system's worked a lot better because it has provided more flexibility and I'm not torn between the two goals. I find I'm more efficient at the office because when I do stay late, I can complete a major chunk of work. I also find that the quality of the time spent at home is improved because I focus on being there.

By working as late as needed some nights and then coming home at a set time on other nights, this dad has improved the balance in his life. He has set realistic expectations for his family and is living up to them. As importantly, he's meeting his personal standards for the quality of his work.

Since there is always the promise of a break coming up, pulsing helps you get through rough days at work, as this office worker found:

> When I have one of those very difficult days overflowing with meetings (probably 3 days per week), I remind myself that tomorrow I have scheduled a departure time that will allow me some time with my family. I apply the pulsing principle during my workday as well. About twice a week I take a lunch out of the office and go somewhere and go over all the reading material that's important but not urgent. I enjoy being alone and casually going through my work.

Pulsing also helps alleviate those vague feelings of contrition we sometimes have when we don't keep a workaholic's schedule:

> I've been using the concept of pulsing regularly. It helps me to prioritize my time. Knowing I am working late allows me to ease my mind so on other days when I leave early/on time, I don't feel guilty about doing so.

The strategy of pulsing works best when you force yourself into a more or less predictable schedule. In the first place, having a pattern of working late on specified nights makes it easier to say "No" to requests to stay late other nights. It also makes arranging nonwork events a lot easier. Scheduling your flamenco dancing lessons or yoga class every Wednesday night is a surer strategy for getting out of the office than a wishy-washy pledge to leave work early to get some exercise.

While I desert the office by 5:30 on most nights, I stay until 7:30 or so every Tuesday. Then I meet my husband for a late dinner at a restaurant near our house. We get home long after the baby-sitter has put the kids to bed. This pulsing approach has made Tuesday one of my favorite days. I dine by candle-light with the man I love. I'm released from supervising the kids' teethbrushing and having to read two different bedtime stories. Oh yes, I also get to catch up with my work. There's no doubt about it; pulsing provides little pleasures that make life sweet.

Phasing: Work Long Days and Then Rest

All rising to a great place is by a winding stair.
Francis Bacon

Sometimes your workload becomes so great that it sucks up any available time and you can't afford the open evenings that pulsing allows. This is when you apply the technique of phas-ing. Phasing is committing to lengthy workdays for several weeks, or maybe even months, but scheduling a definite date when you will return to reasonable hours.

Starting a new job is a classic situation where phasing is required. You have lots to learn, new responsibilities, and per-haps the urge to impress the new boss with your sterling qual-ities. In jobs that have seasonal spikes, phasing may become an annual event. Tax offices are a good example. In most account-ing firms the work starts to build in December and becomes overwhelming by the end of March and early April. No matter how much you've proselytized the value of balance, you won't win any popularity contests if you leave exactly on time during those busy periods. With phasing, you can put in the long hours, knowing the workload will slack by May and you can regain a more balanced schedule at that point.

Be Conscious of Your Trade-offs

I have found it is much easier to make a success in life
than to make a success of one's life.
G. W. Follin

If you have to enter an extended period with a heavy workload, don't blind yourself to what you are choosing and what the implications are. We all face the risk of being seduced into a demanding work schedule without understanding the consequences. At first the new responsibilities are just a little more work, then they balloon into a bit more, and suddenly there's an enormous workload towering over you. Yet somehow you have committed yourself and have to complete it all.

So if you know or even suspect you are about to enter a heavy work phase, ask yourself these questions:

1. Why do I want to do this? What is motivating me?
2. Realistically, how long a commitment am I making?
3. What is the probability that the time frame will be extended? If it is extended, what will I do? Am I comfortable with that?
4. What will I have to take off my schedule in order to work these hours? Am I comfortable with that?

5. Does anyone else (i.e., my family) need to be involved with this decision? How much am I willing to let their preferences shape my decision?

Once you are satisfied with your answers to these questions and decide to enter a heavy work phase, here are a few survival techniques you might find helpful.

Staying Balanced While Phasing

The winds of grace are always flowing, but you have to raise the sail.
Ramakrishna

To maintain some balance when you're in heavy work phase, you first need to decide which of your Personal Priorities mean the most to you. Which ones can you spend less time on, even if not as much as you would like? Are there any you will have to shelve completely during this phase? Which ones should you continue to nurture? Even if you decide to neglect some of your priorities, you'll feel better for having made the choice, as did this Balanced Life class attendee:

I'm in a start-up mode right now with new responsibilities so I'm not spending as much time with my husband and baby as I would like. However, the Personal Priority and the "What motivates me?" exercises left me with a very strong sense that having a balanced life is totally up to me. I live knowing that everything I do is a choice—my choice. Ironically, knowing that makes me feel better about not being with my family because I am consciously making my decisions.

The second technique to make phasing more manageable is to pay homage to your Personal Priorities in small ways. No matter how demanding your work schedule, there will be some amount of free time. Waste that time on frivolous distractions and the work world will eventually conquer you. But if you take advantage of pauses in the action to clasp one of your Personal Priorities, you will know you are still pointing your life in the direction you want.

Sometimes even a minute or two is enough to explore and refresh the nonwork priorities of your life. Here are a few examples of how you can spend time on your Personal Priorities while still working 60-, 70-, or even 80-hour weeks.

- *If Your Priority Is "Being Healthy":* Do a couple of stretches for your neck and shoulders while waiting for a red light. Breathe deep and let some of that tension release.
- *If Your Priority Is "Being Creative":* Stuck on a problem? Grab some colored pens or pencils and spend five minutes drawing the problem using symbols, arrows, etc. Let your mind wander while you contemplate your drawing and see what new ideas come to you.
- *If Your Priority Is "Giving to My Community":* As you sort through your mail at the end of a long day, keep your eyes open for a solicitation from a charity that appeals to you. Stop immediately and write them a check, even if it's only a small one.
- *If Your Priority Is "Having a Close Family":* Leave a love note for your family to read in the evening when you are not home. Or call your home answering machine to say, "I miss you."
- *If Your Priority Is "Developing My Spirituality":* Say a

prayer or practice a loving-kindness meditation during your commute.

- *If Your Priority Is "Being Generous to Others"*: On your run to the vending machine, pick up three or four items and share them with your co-workers.

Integrating your Priorities into overly busy days will remind you that you honor aspects of life other than work. You'll have a better perspective on your job, reducing the stress and panic that sometimes overtake people when they are in the middle of a major assignment. You'll find that spending time on your Personal Priorities helps you be more effective at your work, by stoking your enthusiasm for the life you want to lead.

The third tactic for successful phasing is to establish an end date. Then do everything in your power to keep it. If you are part of a project, it's apt to have a deadline. Use that as a rallying point to motivate yourself and others to be done with it by then. If there is no external deadline (for example, you are in the process of learning a new job), then impose a deadline on yourself and commit to it. A good way to do that is to schedule an event which will mark the end of your heavy work phase. Plan a vacation, or even a long weekend, to celebrate crossing the finish line. Make reservations and put down some hefty deposits. As the end point approaches, you'll have a constant reminder of your promise to yourself and lots of incentive to keep it.

This lawyer found that planning an end date helped her through some difficult times:

When I started in a new job, I thought a lot about the "phasing" notion. I scheduled a vacation so that it would happen

right after the conclusion of some major contract negotiations.
I went to a spa and relaxed for a week—it was really wonder-
ful and just what I needed. The "phasing" approach certainly
kept me sane and motivated because it helped me realize that
the craziness was not something I had to sustain endlessly.

Using Phasing to Advance Your Ambition

Happiness is a way station between too little and too much.
Channing Pollock

Phasing is a very effective strategy for ambitious people who want balance while still progressing in their careers. Frequently, you prove yourself to an organization by accepting challenging assignments and demonstrating positive results in short periods of time. Phasing is a creative compromise that allows you to accept this type of assignment and not make long-term trade-offs. However, be careful. If you allow time-consuming assignments to follow one after another, you are no longer phasing. You're making significant lifestyle trade-offs, but unconsciously, which is the worst possible way.

Sometimes attempts at phasing involve trade-offs that people later regret. One ambitious man described his undertaking this way:

I knew this assignment was going to be totally time consum-
ing so I told my kids not to expect me to be around a lot for
the next six months. Unfortunately, the project dragged on
and six months turned into nine months. It was as if I went
into a tunnel and didn't come out. Every now and then my
kids still refer to that period and call it "the time Daddy wasn't

here." *If I had it to do over, I would do something else. My family and I paid too high a price.*

The hard question for this man to answer is, what would he have done instead? Not accept the assignment and perhaps slow down his career advancement? Quit after the first six months when the project didn't finish on time? Neither seems likely. Perhaps his best option, and yours should you ever be in a similar situation, would be to accept the assignment but be strongly committed to eking out some time for Personal Priorities, no matter how grueling the workload. Taking momentary breaks and continuing to grant yourself a regular evening off may be the best long-term approach to achieve your work goals and minimize your regrets.

Coping with a Demanding Boss

Let your workings remain a mystery. Just show people the results.
Tao Te Ching

As I have been describing pulsing and phasing, it has been under the assumption that your motivation to work long hours is coming from within. But sometimes you and your boss may disagree on how many hours you should devote to work. You may be asking yourself how you're going to maintain some balance in your life if you have to work all the hours that he or she demands.

You can use either pulsing or phasing as a tactic to clock up some hours and appease your boss. Depressingly, that additional time may be more for show than what is really required by the job. This mother of two, in one of her first professional jobs out of college, had this experience:

> I was very efficient at the office and usually got my work done, so I would leave every evening at 5. If I didn't get everything done, I would come in early because that's what worked with my child care. Then one day a woman co-worker told me that our boss was insinuating that I wasn't dedicated or ambitious. She suggested that I work past 5 more often. When I explained why I didn't she was very frank and said that if I wanted to been seen as a "player," I had to be here in the evenings. So I arranged a baby-sitter for one night a week and worked late. I resented it, but it did seem to help me be more accepted.

Because some bosses stubbornly confuse quality time with quantity time, you may have to rely on a certain amount of subterfuge to maintain a rich home life while still progressing in the workplace. I don't advocate outright lying, though. It creates bad karma, and the repercussions can be serious if you get caught. On the other hand, as long as you are getting your work done, a bit of discretion about when you are and are not physically at your workplace might be an acceptable approach. If Wednesday is your night to work late, it doesn't hurt to make sure your boss is aware you're there. But don't announce that every other night you're gone by 5.

Using phone mail and e-mail is another way to create the perception of a particularly long day while you're still able to spend your time on other priorities, as this person has found:

I use the "virtual" phone mail trick pretty frequently and check my messages late in the evening. If I get a message from my boss, I'll send off my reply right away, even if it could easily wait until morning. I admit I do this only to impress her with how dedicated I am. (I am dedicated; I just don't want to be in the office all hours of the night.)

Telling Your Boss You Need More Balance

Go out on the limb—that's where the fruit is.
Will Rogers

You may face a situation where a combination of pulsing, phasing, and discretion doesn't seem to be working. It could be that your boss's prejudices, the norms of your corporate culture, and/or the requirements of your job truly preclude you from having a balanced life. Before resigning yourself to a workaholic's schedule, however, it is worth discussing your desire for balance with your boss. Be sure you are well prepared—this is not a conversation you want to ad-lib. Most importantly, you want to focus on the goals you and your higher-up share, specifically to create a better quality work product. Then you need to discuss whether there are other ways of achieving that work product short of investing long hours. Point out the advantages of the various timesaving techniques and how you have used them to increase your personal productivity. Suggest that if he could get the same quality haircut in thirty minutes as he could in sixty minutes, he would go to the more efficient barber. Shouldn't that same logic apply to his employees?

When this operations manager decided she had to discuss balance with her supervisor, the conversation went better than she expected:

Although my boss and I have different lifestyles and motivators, he supports balance more than I would have imagined. The initiative behind the discussion was I had to announce my pregnancy to him. I tried hard to focus the discussion on results and that was helpful. Although I have always been results oriented, I haven't always communicated that as clearly as I could. By taking the focus away from working hours and placing it on effectiveness, our conversation went very well.

To help support your arguments with your boss, look at the chart here. The first column shows how many good workers approach their jobs. The middle column describes how great workers approach their jobs by delegating, prioritizing, and having a broad perspective. By a happy coincidence, people who value balance think like the great workers. They also rely on delegating, prioritizing, and having a broad perspective. Balanced-life types are highly motivated to use different and more creative approaches to getting the work done. After all, they want to go home.

To the degree you can articulate to your boss how your desire for reasonable hours can be used to the company's benefit, the better your chances for negotiating a bargain you'll both be happy with. Hopefully, you'll find your boss is the perceptive type who can recognize the benefit of measuring results rather than hours worked. Some people are not so lucky, as shown by this marketing analyst who attended one of my Balanced Life courses:

HOW MANY GOOD WORKERS APPROACH THEIR JOBS	HOW MANY GREAT WORKERS APPROACH THEIR JOBS	THE BALANCED LIFE PERSPECTIVE
How do I get my co-workers/ employees to work harder?	How do I get my co-workers/ employees to be more creative problem solvers?	When the people who work with me work creatively, we all benefit from better results in less time.
What is the best way to deal with this emergency?	How do we avoid this emergency in the future?	Emergencies are wasteful of time and energy. Let's do the forward thinking we need to keep them to a minimum.
How do I keep staffing low to control the expenses in my unit?	What's the most cost-efficient way to deliver quality?	In the long run, simplifying, prioritizing, and eliminating work are far more cost effective than trying to get people to work harder and longer.
If I do this myself, I know it will be done quickly and with good quality.	Who can do this task as well as or better than I can? Who can do this task as well as I can after some training?	By delegating interesting work to others, I make their jobs more rewarding, help the company develop its human resources, and free up my schedule for other priorities.
How do I get my co-workers/ employees to work longer hours?	How do I get my co-workers/ employees committed to achieving business goals?	Results are better when we focus the goals and outcomes rather than the process of getting there.

I am finding it difficult to achieve more balance, since my supervisor still measures dedication by the number of hours spent in the evening, at the office. She doesn't get in until 9 in the morning. If I come in and work early that doesn't count because she doesn't see me. Working at home doesn't count either. The situation is frustrating, but it has been helpful for me to realize that the power resides within me to make choices about how I want to spend my time. Even though my supervisor and I have very different views of this, I feel confident (and not guilty) about making my choices.

This woman has decided to choose her work hours without catering to all the dictates of her manager. With my perpetual desire to please, I would never be gutsy enough to openly challenge my supervisor's authority like she did, but it is an option that can be picked by other, more courageous souls.

You may eventually come to an impasse in your current job, when your desire for balance conflicts so much with your workplace that the situation is unsustainable. What to do in that case? It might be time to look for a new job. As more employers are competing for capable employees, they are becoming much more flexible regarding balance issues. Your mission will be to find a job you like that will also allow you to live the life you want. How to change jobs to find more balance is discussed in detail in Chapter 12.

Exploration Exercises

Looking in the Mirror
The key to managing either a pulsing or a phasing strategy successfully is to be committed to sticking with whatever schedule you establish. Obviously, there'll need to be some flexibility, but if you find your two "work-late" nights expand into four or that the six months required to learn a new job stretches into twelve, then you are no longer pulsing or phasing. You are just working too many hours and potentially losing your sense of balance. To try to prevent that from occurring, do these exercises when you contemplate moving to a pulsing or phasing schedule:

1. What might motivate you to break your commitment to your pulsing or phasing schedule? Review Chapter 3 and

determine what motivators might be most apt to separate you from your ideal plan. How can you strengthen your resolve and resist that pressure?

2. Review the Ambition Trade-off Chart at the end of Chapter 4. Thinking about the period during which you will be pulsing or phasing, write down the answers to these questions:

- What am I willing to trade off from the areas of time, relationships, geography, and core principles during this time?
- What am I not willing to trade off?
- With whom should I be discussing my decisions?

Review your answers to these questions every week or so to make sure you are not sliding into a workaholic pit.

Commute Questions

(These questions are for you to ponder when you are commuting, waiting in line, etc. Think of them as directed daydreams.)

- As you commute back and forth during these long days, ask yourself how you might still devote time, even just a few moments a day, to your Personal Priorities. You will find that even temporary pauses from your work will refresh you and make you feel more in control. Refer back to page 103 for some ideas to get you started.
- If you are in a very heavy work phase and you have planned some mini-breaks, try to develop a plan on how you can take an extra evening off in the next two weeks. Spend that time on your most favorite Personal Priority.

Action Step

On your calendar, write down a work schedule that incorporates either pulsing or phasing. If you opt for pulsing, be sure to respect the nights you are not going to be working by devoting them to your other Priorities. If you choose phasing, pick the end date and plan an event or mini-vacation to celebrate your return to a normal schedule.

> To me, having a balanced life means not looking back and having regrets—knowing I have always had ample time to be an active participant in my family, and not just a tired parent showing up barely in time for dinner.
>
> A middle-aged compensation executive and father of two teenagers

Whose Rules Make You Work So Much?

A CHILD'S QUESTION

A little boy asks his father why he always brings home so much work in his briefcase.

"It is for my job," his father answers. "I can't get it all done during the day."

"Gosh, Daddy," replies his son. "Can't they just put you in a slower class?"

What is your excuse for working so many hours?

Is there a force other than ambition that drives you to work so many hours? Did you read and understand the guiding principles for balance in Chapter 5 yet still don't honor your departure hour? Did your attempts at pulsing or phasing fail because you couldn't force yourself to take a break? What keeps you on the job as twilight darkens the sky? What compels you to return to an uninhabited office on a Saturday? Why do you labor at home long after your spouse and children are asleep?

Who's to Blame, Your Job or You?

You never expected justice from a company, did you? They have
neither a soul to lose, nor a body to kick.
Sydney Smith

Any size organization, from minute to mammoth, might demand grueling workdays from its employees. You may have just launched your own company where long hours are needed to get the business going. Or you may be in a small start-up firm where endless days are expected as the "dues" for a successful business and delightfully lucrative stock offering. Within a large firm, your department may have recently been shattered by a series of layoffs. Suddenly there is more work to be done by fewer people and the threat of losing your job is only too real. So you work more hours.

Maybe you work in a profession that bills by the hour. The more hours you work, the more revenue you earn. In these circumstances, you have a minimum number of hours that have to be billed and the number may translate into workweeks that are far north of forty hours.

If you work on an hourly basis, mandatory overtime or shift changes can prevent you from having the time you need for yourself. For when the boss says you have to come in to work, you have to come in to work.

In other words, there are hundreds of possible circumstances where you might feel trapped into working long hours where even pulsing or phasing offer no relief. It's a mistake, however, to point a blaming finger at your work situation and say it's *entirely* responsible for the number of hours you work. You can't convince me that some warden is locking chains on your ankle when you go to work in the morning and then refusing to let you free before midnight. If you're working extremely long hours, then you're imprisoned by someone's expectations. The expectations may emanate from your boss. Or they may come from some internal directive that you embraced many years ago.

If these expectations come exclusively from your boss or the true demands of your business, then you either have to accept your fate or start looking for a new job. (I'd urge you to try the second approach, and Chapter 12 has suggestions on how to go about it.) However, if the pressure for working endless hours is coming primarily from you, it's time to admit that you're perpetuating a workaholic situation. Some inner compulsion prevents you from adhering to the guiding principles of a balanced life: (1) making good use of your time, (2) leaving at a departure hour, and (3) saying "No" to requests not related to your Personal Priorities. Instead, you may find you're contending for one of three spurious goals: pursuing perfection, searching for enough, or striving for completion.

Pursuing Perfection

The intellect of man is forced to choose
Perfection of the life, or of the work.
W. B. Yeats

Women seem to be particularly smitten by the desire for perfection. For many women and some men, what they do never seems to be quite good enough. There's always something more that could be written, some conclusion that needs further proof, or some presentation that requires better graphics. Frequently, this search for perfection distorts the significance of the actual work. Relatively routine tasks grow to major undertakings as the creator strives to fix the flaws that are only visible to her. A supervisor tells of one situation:

> I am struggling with an employee who is always striving to be perfect. Her desire to have flawless analyses and presentations drives her co-workers and subordinates crazy. She has trouble recruiting staff to her area. Deadlines are barely made or missed altogether as she tries to make everything impeccable. Her search for perfectionism is actually lowering the quality of her work. I have told her, "Stop trying to be a 98% player in an 85% world." I'm not sure she hears me.

What does it mean to be a "98% player in an 85% world"? It means you are devoting your valuable hours to improvements that no one else cares about. Every work environment has certain elements that have to be done perfectly. And each workplace has many more elements that require only superficial attention. Take a look at your work environment and learn where it matters to be perfect and where it doesn't. Then stop spending time striving to perfect stuff no one else appreciates. After all, you don't iron your underwear, do you?

Relentless striving for perfection might also indicate a supersensitivity to criticism. Sometimes perfectionists fear disapproval so much that they will go to any length to avoid it. "As long as my work is perfect," the logic goes, "no one can ever accuse me of doing a bad job." This quest for the irreproachable is a flawed one, of course, as the effort required to achieve perfection in one endeavor always results in shortcomings in another. At some point, you have to be able to say, "My work is fine the way it is. Putting in extra hours isn't going to make it that much better."

Pushing Back on Perfectionism

I have had more trouble with myself than with any person
I have ever met.
Dwight Moody

The following story tells of a woman who was forced to be less of a perfectionist for a while:

A few months ago, I was hit by a car while crossing the street and had to reduce my work schedule significantly. Normally, I worked 50- to 60-hour weeks, making sure everything was done perfectly to my standards. After the accident, I had to let others do more of the work. I was very uncomfortable about this at first and afraid the quality would go down. But after a while, I realized that the end product was as good as or better than if I had put in all those extra hours. My boss was totally satisfied and my staff was more energized then they had ever been. Too bad it took such a painful lesson to teach me that my perfectionism wasn't worth it.

If you find yourself wrestling with perfectionism, choose an area of your work and relax your standards for a while. See if anyone notices. If that approach is too unsettling for you, then get an objective reading from a peer or even your boss. Ask them what they value in your work and why. You need to understand if your standards are compatible with those of your organization.

If none of these techniques work, remind yourself how the Book of Genesis describes God's evaluation of His work as He created the world: *And God saw that it was good.* Not perfect, good. And then on the seventh day, instead of going back to try to make everything perfect, God rested. You should too.

Searching for Enough

Perpetual devotion to what a person calls his business is only to be sustained by perpetual neglect of many other things.
Robert Louis Stevenson

If your job is like most of the jobs in America, you always have the sense that no matter how much you do, someone is always wanting more. "More widgets, more paper, more output," a voice demands. Whether that voice comes from a boss, a peer, a customer, or from inside our own heads, our reaction tends to be the same—to work more hours.

But since working more hours robs us of our opportunity for a balanced life, what's another way of responding to that demanding voice? One way is to ask, "How much is enough?"

It is surprisingly difficult for most people to define what enough is. How much is enough money? More than I have. How much is enough respect? More than I have. How much is enough love? Alas, more than I have. Surveys that ask people how much more they need to earn to be financially comfortable inevitably come up with the same answer. It is 20% to 40% more than they make right now. It doesn't matter if the responder makes $30,000 or $100,000 a year. Enough is more than we have.

When you don't know how to set a limit on how much is "enough" in your life, you become caught up in compulsive behaviors. People who eat too much, drink too much, or work too much are incapable of drawing their own limits. They succumb to the insatiable demands of their obsessions, trapped in a tar pit where enough is never enough.

Avoiding the "Never Enough" Trap

We have met the enemy and he is us.
Pogo (Walt Kelly)

How do you create the boundary of "enough" in your work situation? The first step is to realize that in most cases, no one but you will even acknowledge the need for a boundary. Those people that consistently yammer "more, more, more" don't know how to utter "enough." Therefore, you have to set that limit for yourself. Second, you need to realize that whether you work forty hours a week or a hundred, the demand for more work will probably never be satisfied. Picture yourself at a beach. You've dug a hole in the sand and now are trying to fill it with water. How much water is enough to fill the hole? There isn't enough; the sand will always suck the hole dry. Too often, work situations are like a hole in the sand. No matter how much you do, there will always be the cry for more. So are you still scurrying across the hot beach with a sloshing bucket trying to replenish a perpetually empty hole? If so, you have only yourself to blame for the inevitable frustration and exhaustion.

The third key to keeping out of the "never enough" trap is to acknowledge that it is easier for you to say "I could do more" than it is to say "I have done enough." The fact is, you can almost always do more, no matter how much you've already accomplished. Deciding to do more requires zero judgment. However, to know when you have done enough does require judgment. And if you are a person who believes you can never do enough, then your judgment has limited use in this situation, as this Balanced Life student attests:

> The idea of never doing enough really hit home for me. I want to be perceived as the "good soldier" and that seems to mean I should keep on working, even if it's not the best way to act all the time. I can't seem to get away from the perception that there is always more to do.

To avoid this dilemma, try to evaluate your work through another person's eyes. This person should have reasonable standards for quality, but those standards should be less strict than your own. In other words, it should *not* be your mother. Imagine this person was assessing what you had done during the day. Would it be considered adequate? If you think it would earn his or her endorsement, then tell yourself you have done enough. Go home and start to work on your Personal Priorities.

Yet another approach is to recognize that there'll be times when you won't be able to do everything you'd like. Setting priorities, whether they're your work priorities or your Personal Priorities, means that some things you care about will go wanting. Accept that fact. Find a way to handle the important issues and ignore the rest. Listen to how one department manager dealt with demands on her time:

I looked at my calendar and realized it was a totally crazy time. There were three evening events all in the same week. Enough is enough, I thought, and decided which two were the most important. I skipped the third one, a retirement dinner for a man I had worked with. I was careful to call him and say I was wishing him well even if I couldn't come to the party. I was sorry to miss the dinner, but it was more important for me to be at the other events and I just can't do everything.

Were some people disappointed that this manager didn't make her third event? Probably. Did they want more of her time? Yes. Can she give her time to everyone that wants more? No. To have a balanced life means making choices and those choices will inevitably disappoint or even anger some people. It is unfortunate, but true. For you can't have a balanced life and always make everyone happy, particularly those who don't know the difference between more and enough.

Striving for Completion

We can't all do everything.
Virgil

Late at night, a common excuse cascades through the corridors and cubicles of many American companies: "I'll go home as soon as my work is done." Even though this is a noble and principled statement, it's a poor reason to ignore your Personal Priorities. Each of us always has work that is incomplete and we should be thankful for that. Since we didn't complete everything today, that means there is still a job for us tomorrow. In the interest of continued employment, we should be delighted that our work is never ending.

If you're staying late every night to finish your work, ask yourself what type of work is holding you up. Is it truly important or is it merely tying up the loose ends of hundreds of little tasks? Remember the lesson of the relative value of an extra hour and remind yourself that you're extending your workday by about 10% while decreasing your evening hours by half. Is that what you want? Is the value of the hour you'll spend completing that work truly more meaningful than spending an hour on your Personal Priorities?

The excuse that you are working late until everything is "complete" is sometimes a cover-up for less-than-ideal work habits. If you are prioritizing appropriately, then you know what's important to your job and are getting that done during normal working hours. When it's time for your departure hour, there'll be only the less important tasks left, ones you can easily postpone, eliminate, or handle by some other timesaving technique. Aim to leave at your departure hour and you'll discover that you'll work more effectively, as this project manager testifies:

> I'm trying to leave earlier (i.e., 6 rather than 7 . . . well, it is a start) and I find that by having my departure hour as a "deadline," I am far more productive at work. I want to leave and I want to complete my work, so I stay focused.

On the other hand, if you find you still have to work unusually long hours even after you prioritize, you might be in a different kind of situation. It might be that you're plagued with last-minute "emergencies," you're in desperate need of some quiet time, or you are flat-out overloaded. Each of these situations is manageable once you identify the problem.

Regain Control and Then Go Home

Be thine own palace, or the world's thy jail.
John Donne

"Something else came up" is a common excuse for not completing important work during the day. Maybe you're in a workplace where emergencies frequently flutter down like confetti, requiring all employees to grab their brooms and help with the cleanup. What are those emergencies that keep dropping from the sky? Are they more or less critical than what you had planned to accomplish? If you're dealing with a serious crisis that depends solely on your heroic efforts, you may have to work late. But consider how often these unanticipated events interfere with your normal work. If they descend on you daily or even weekly, then they should no longer be unexpected. Figure out some approaches to forestall these "emergencies." Then you can hang on to your balance, as this administrative assistant did:

At the end of the day, my boss was always giving me a big pile of stuff that had to be done by morning. I finally got sick of working late while he went home so I started asking him around 4 o'clock what he wanted me to do before the end of the day. It was a gentle reminder that I had a life, too. It didn't always work, but it made the situation a lot better.

The need for uninterrupted time also surfaces as a rationale for working late to complete important tasks. Some people believe that the only way to have quiet time is to outlast every other employee. As more and more people spend their work hours in open-air cubicles, private time is as rare as a perfect blind date. But do you really have to stay later than the other workers to find some peace and quiet, or would you get the same results if you could work somewhere that other people weren't? Can you go home early and work there for an hour or two when you need to be alone? Or could you sneak off to an empty conference room? Or maybe create a virtual quiet zone by turning off your phone, slapping on some headphones, and brushing off all visitors?

A production assistant developed this method for creating quiet time for herself:

> *Working in a cubicle makes it tough to concentrate on what I need to get done. Then one day I strung a strip of tape across the opening to my cube and put up a* DO NOT DISTURB *sign. A few people "pretended" not to notice, but I was very clear with them that I had a lot to do and they should go away if it wasn't urgent. I found the sign also worked for me—just knowing it was there helped me not be distracted by other issues.*

Finally, you might be in a situation where you are so overloaded with critical tasks that even periods of pulsing or phasing don't allow you to accomplish what must be done. If so, then someone, either the boss or you, is setting unrealistic expectations for your job. If you ever want time for your other priorities, you have to reset these expectations. Otherwise, you'll be like Sisyphus, who was condemned to spend eternity pushing a rock up a hill only to have it roll down again once he reached the top. If you think the day's work is never complete, then you're caught in a similar never-ending cycle and you'll never find your balance.

Abandon Those Spurious Pursuits

"Why aren't you dancing with joy at this very moment?" is the only relevant spiritual question.
Pir Vilayer Khan

Pursuing perfection, seeking enough, and longing for completion are all common and understandable human behaviors. In and of themselves, there is nothing wrong with them. But when applied to your work life, they can create barriers between you and your other Personal Priorities—especially the first two, which may be admirable but are generally unobtainable. Even striving for completion is deceptive. For as we pass one milestone, isn't there yet another one ahead of us?

If you want to bow out of these particular pursuits, recognize that your work habits, your attitude, or your work environment will have to change. So start experimenting. For one week, try walking out the door with your work imperfect, inadequate, or incomplete. See if the consequences are as excruciating as you imagined. And if the strategies I've suggested don't work, perhaps you should consider changing jobs so you have a workplace that supports rather than resists your need for balance.

Take heart. You will eventually choose to preserve your time for your Personal Priorities. You just have to keep trying until you find the door that opens for you.

Exploration Exercises

Looking in the Mirror

As you think about leaving work at a set departure hour so you have time for other Personal Priorities, which of these reasons might motivate you to stay later? (If you check more than one, try to put them in rank order.)

- The obligation to accomplish a certain amount in a given day.
- The desire to complete the project you are working on.
- The sense that everyone else is working late, too.
- The desire for quiet or unscheduled time.
- The sense that it will help your job advancement.
- The thought that you have no other pressing engagements outside of work.
- Something else?

What are some ways you can modify either your workday or your attitude so there are fewer barriers between you and your departure hour?

Commute Questions

(These questions are for you to ponder when you are commuting, waiting in line, etc. Think of them as directed daydreams.)

- As you go into work in the morning, decide what time you want to leave and make that your departure hour for the day. Review your five Personal Priorities and choose one that will benefit from the time you will create by leaving work at your departure hour. Imagine how pleasant it will be to do something you really care about other than work.

- On your way home, check the time. Are you pleased with when you left the workplace? If it is later than you'd like, review your day and see if there were opportunities when you might have used one of the six time-savers. If you are pleased with the time you left, congratulate yourself on creating more balance in your life.

Action Step

Establish your own departure hour. Choose a time that is reasonable for you to stop your work and will still give you hours to spend on other priorities. Aim to leave at that hour at least two out of the next five work nights. Write it down on your calendar. Write it in a contract with yourself and sign it. Tell your co-workers you have commitments for those evenings and therefore have to leave by a certain time. If you have a family, tell them to expect you home earlier than usual. Take a travel alarm clock to work with you and set it, your digital watch, or your computer's clock to go off at the departure hour. When the alarm goes off, leave.

This exercise also works well with a partner. Since you will be asking this partner to check up on you periodically, be sure it is someone who can gently nag you without provoking any defensive reactions. (Your spouse may not be the best choice.) Ask him or her to call you at the office a few minutes after your departure hour. If you are still there, that is your signal to go home.

To me, having a balanced life means feeling like I have given 100% to both work and home—jeez, no wonder I'm exhausted!

A middle manager in a computer systems department who is also the mother of two toddlers

E-mail, Phone Mail, Pagers: Who Is in Control?

> ## WALKING THE DOG
>
> A boy and a girl are walking their dogs in the park. The boy's dog is very rambunctious, dragging him back and forth across the grass. When the girl's pooch tries to wander too far afield, she tugs on its leash and guides the animal back to the path. At last, the girl decides to give some advice to the boy.
>
> "Listen," she says. "Your dog walks in front of you and he may think he is leading you on that leash. But you have to show him who's boss. You need to convince him that you have more control at your end of the leash than he does at his."

*When you think of the electronic communications devices you use,
who has the control? You or the person on the other end of the line?*

Have you ever been about to start a relaxed lunch with a friend and a cellular phone starts ringing from the depths of some briefcase? Does your pager go off just as you are pulling into the health club's parking lot? Do you sneak into your home office on Saturdays to do your e-mail, hoping the family won't discover you there?

When you first thought about getting a cell phone, pager, or e-mail, did you think they would make your life better or worse? And which has it been, better or worse?

The truth probably is both. The communication technologies popularized in the 1990s have been a double-edged sword. On the one hand, they facilitate rapid and generally more accurate communications. Phone mail allows customers to leave detailed messages without having to go through a receptionist. E-mail makes it a snap to deliver a written message to dozens of people located all over the world. In case of an emergency, pagers allow others to find us day or night.

The negative side of these communications, however, has to do with the changing expectations that come along with them. If Mr. Peterson leaves you a message on phone mail, he knows that you know he needs to talk to you. So why haven't you called him back? Since it's so easy to send out e-mails, Mary puts you on the distribution list of her latest proposal. And she does expect a response back in less than twenty-four hours—after all, there is no delivery time issue. Now that your boss has your pager number, he feels free to use it whenever he think it's an emergency. And since you haven't answered his e-mail after two hours, he's getting irritated and believes this situation constitutes an emergency.

Don't Let Your Messages Dominate Your Life

There is an unlucky tendency . . . to allow every new invention to add to life's complications, and every new power to increase life's hustling; so that, unless we can dominate the mischief, we are really the worse off instead of the better.

Vernon Lee

As I have mentioned before, one of the prerequisites to having balance in your life is to feel like you control your own time. But nothing interrupts that sense of control like the rhythmic beep-beeping of some electronic device demanding your immediate attention. Few of us are strong enough to resist that siren call. Either our sense of obligation or our curiosity is too strong for us to ignore the outcry. But once we pick up the phone, read the pager's display, or open up our e-mail, we have surrendered our control to whoever is on the other end of the digital highway, as this man seems to have done:

> I have absolutely no system on how to control these things. I am constantly checking my voice mail, calling in five to six times a day, even while on vacation. I also have my cell phone with me all the time. Fortunately I haven't gotten caught up in the world of pagers yet, so that's the only thing that saves me there!

So how to avoid falling into that trap without declaring all electronic communications taboo? There are many approaches you can use. The overall objective for each, however, is to make yourself the master of your messages, not the other way around. The ways you can reexert control are restricting when you access your messages, developing screening techniques, and setting others' expectations on how you respond to the messages they leave you.

Keep the Interruptions Confined

Have you ever noticed that life consists mostly of interruptions, with
occasional spells of rush work in between?
Buwei Yang Chao

Purveyors of electronic communications devices try to seduce us with advertising that promises access to our messages any time, anywhere. While it is true you can now communicate virtually all the time and from everywhere, you don't have to respond immediately to every interruption transmitted by those contraptions. If you want balance in your life, let your electronic gizmos give you the ability to *choose* the time and the place you communicate with others. Unlike the photos in the ads, you probably won't choose to exchange messages with your work colleagues while walking along a beach at sunset. I'm confident that you'll pick a more practical approach for talking to the office and reserve your beach walks for more soul-satisfying purposes.

Picking certain periods of the day to deal with your messages is a very effective way to reestablish control over your electronics. By doing this, you stay focused on the task at hand without being interrupted by incoming missives of varying degrees of importance and urgency. You'll work more efficiently and maybe even achieve your goal of leaving by your departure hour. Plus, when you're not racing through a message to get back to some other chore, your responses can be more thoughtful.

Different people find that different intervals and times of the day work best for them when it comes to responding to messages. It might take some experimenting to find the pattern that works for you. You may also find it hard to restrain yourself from peeking at your messages at any other time. If you need suggestions, here are some ideas from attendees of my Balanced Life classes.

A mother with young children writes,

> I log on to my home PC at 6 or 6:30 A.M., answer e-mail and phone mail for an hour or so, then wake everyone up. I have to do this or my office day is cluttered with my thinking that I need to respond to everything in a timely fashion. These early morning sessions add another one to two hours to my workday, but it is time that the family doesn't miss.

This self-employed consultant has another approach:

> I dedicate specific time each morning and each afternoon for my e-mail . . . as opposed to being its slave and watching it all the time. Toward that end I have shut off any audibles [the beeping or chirping signals that some e-mail systems send out when a new message arrives in your in-box] that alert me to the arrival of a mail item. If I don't know it's there, it is a lot easier to ignore.

A message from a reformed voice mail junkie:

> I definitely allowed voice mail to control my life, phoning in every hour. Now, I'll check in twice, at noon and at the end of the day. At the end of the day, if there is nothing tagged urgent, I don't even listen to my messages, because that means it is nothing that can't be handled tomorrow.

And another idea:

In addition to checking for messages once or twice during the day, I always check my voice mail about 10 at night. I'll return messages or make a note to myself to follow up the next morning. This approach has two advantages. When I clear out my voice mail late at night, usually there are no messages waiting for me when I come in the next day. This makes my mornings seem much calmer. Also, when people get a voice mail from me late at night, they think I am so dedicated to work. In fact, I never think about work between the time I leave my office and the time I make my late night check-in.

Maybe you object to delayed message checking because you feel you're being rude when you don't deal with another person's concerns immediately. A fact you might forget is that the people who send you e-mail or phone mail don't know if you're sitting at your desk ignoring their messages or if you're out of the office and simply unaware that the messages are there. So use their ignorance to your advantage and answer all messages according to your schedule and not the dictates of others.

Don't Check in During Vacations

Only in the oasis of silence can we drink deeply from our inner cup of wisdom.
Sue Patton Thoele

Another important time boundary is to resist picking up messages while on vacation. If you're serious about having balance in your life, you need to take occasional and total breaks from your work life. Checking in to get your messages keeps you mentally shackled to your job at just the time you should be liberating yourself. So leave your pager behind and after leaving appropriate notifications, turn off your phone mail and e-mail. Let one trusted individual know how to contact you in case of a true emergency and go off to spend time on your other Priorities.

When I preach this "vacations are off-limits" discipline in my Balanced Life courses, I generally hear a lot of objections. But after discussing the problems and sharing ideas, people learn that in most cases, they can disengage while on vacation without any serious consequences. Here is one lawyer's experience:

> The first time I turned off my voice mail was last year when I went to India for three weeks. Because I was gone for so long, I would have gotten a lot of messages that would have been completely obsolete by the time I listened to them. So, I turned it off and it made returning to the office so much easier—no old voice mails to go through and get tense about, and, more importantly, people who called knew I wasn't accessible. Now I turn it off even when I am gone for just a few days, and I leave the name of a backup person who knows how to contact me in case it is an emergency.

A sales agent used the concept of a backup person to make sure her clients were well served during her vacation:

> I used to think I had to check in daily even while on vacation to make sure no customers were trying to reach me. But then I realized I could leave a message on my voice mail that gave

the name and contact number of a work friend who could help out or contact me in case of emergency. That way I could shut down my voice mail until I got back. When my friend goes on vacation, I handle her client emergencies for her, so it works out pretty well.

Sometimes you'll encounter resistance from others when you say that you aren't going to be calling in for messages. Remind yourself that people who make those kinds of comments don't appreciate the value of balance. If you feel you must respond, just say there are other parts of your life that need your 100% attention and in a true emergency, your backup knows how to contact you. Then go off and have a good time.

Screen Your Messages

Remember that as a teenager you are at the last stage in your life when you will be happy to hear that the phone is for you.
Fran Lebowitz

We all appreciate what screens do in our homes. They let the fresh air in while keeping the bugs out. When you apply this concept to communication devices, it works in the same way. They let the good stuff through while keeping out the rubbish that bugs you. When skillfully used, electronic communications like phone mail and e-mail come surprisingly close to the bygone secretaries that "screened" calls for their bosses. Like a secretary, e-mail and phone mail delay the immediate delivery of the message to you. Then they create a list of one sort or another of who's contacting you. As you review the list, you get to decide the relative importance of the various messages. Some messages are very important and need to be dealt with immediately. Others are less important and can be postponed until later, delegated to someone else, or even ignored for a few days.

This busy administrator has set up a system that allows him to keep up with the flow of incoming messages while limiting the ones that he responds to immediately:

I structure time into my day to answer e-mail and voice mail, usually at the end of each day. But a couple times during the day, I do check my messages. I generally return only the voice mails marked "urgent," but I also quickly run through the other messages for important "senders." I follow a similar approach on e-mail—scanning any new e-mails for important senders or messages that seem urgent. Those I get back to right away; the rest wait until the end of the day.

Screening is also a useful technique for when you're not at work. Evening phone calls, whether from friends, work colleagues, or telemarketers, interrupt your at-home time and can distract from your Personal Priorities. But you can regain control, as this woman did:

Not answering the phone when I get home has provided me with delicious freedom. My house becomes a refuge where I can enjoy being with my family and shut out the outside world. If someone calls, my answering machine records the message and I'll call back after the kids are asleep. But I only return personal calls at night. My evening times are for me, not my job.

Limit Your Gadgets

The drive towards complex technical achievement offers a clue why
the U.S. is good at space gadgetry and bad at slum problems.
John Kenneth Galbraith

Limiting the variety of communications gadgets you have is another way to screen the number of messages that reach you. Certainly there is prestige in having a cellular phone in your briefcase and a pager clipped to your belt, but do you really need that level of connection? Many people who long for a pager or e-mail access at home later regret their choices as the electronics become overly intrusive. So if you don't currently have every communications contraption, think twice before getting them. They can turn into a mixed blessing, as this person found:

> *I had home e-mail access; however, I stopped that, since it was like a magnet pulling me toward it at every chance it could. Plus, when people got used to my responding to e-mails from home, it became open season on sending me stuff!*

Another example:

> *I stopped wearing a pager. Everyone that wanted to talk to me would just page me regardless of urgency. I also stopped taking my cellular phone in the car with me. It's much safer and it forces me to do my work at work.*

An administrative assistant I know was distressed because her boss wanted her to have a pager so he could reach her after-hours. She felt he was being overly demanding but didn't know how to refuse. If you find yourself in a similar situation, try this approach. Tell your boss that when you're at work, your top priority is work and you try very hard not to let your home life disrupt that. Just as you don't let personal issues interfere with your workday, you don't want work issues disrupting the time you spend away from the office. Therefore, you'd rather not have a pager.

Personally, I hate wearing a pager. Wearing a pager means my boss can track me down whenever he wants, wherever I am. Why in the world would I want that? Besides, I much prefer the illusion of myself as an independent operator, completing what needs to be done in my own way and totally isolated from unwanted interruptions. Luckily, I am also somewhat gadget impaired and never learned (or tried to learn) how to reset a pager or get the messages off it. So I'm comfortable explaining that I didn't get a pager because I don't know how to work the thing. This approach may not work for everyone and it may not work for me forever, but it has served me well over the last few years.

If you don't have the option of refusing a pager or home e-mail, that still doesn't mean you've lost control; you just have to rely on other techniques.

Setting Other People's Expectations

Some things are very important and some are very unimportant.
To know the difference is what we are given life to find out.
Anna F. Trevisan

Many people believe there's a rule somewhere about how quickly one must answer an e-mail or voice mail message. If such a law is written, I haven't been able to find it. E-mail and phone mail are so new in today's business world that no hard and fast rules exist. Many people have opinions about what an appropriate response time is, but that doesn't give them the right to impose their beliefs on you. Instead, you can manage *their* expectations. By letting people know when to anticipate an answer from you, you can liberate your time from the constraint of on-demand communications.

Before you start setting other people's expectations, however, think about your own. After you leave a phone mail or e-mail, how quickly do you expect a response? In one hour, in four hours, by the end of the day? And if the acknowledgment of your message is later than that, how annoyed do you get? No matter what the characteristics of your individual timetable and irritation levels, it is important to realize that they are individual. If you ask around, you'll find that expectations of what creates a "timely" response can vary widely. Usually whatever you define as timely is the standard you try to follow for your own communications.

Because there are no rules about what a reasonable response time is, it's relatively easy to set people's expectations about what to anticipate from you. I used to believe that voice mails should be returned within four hours or less. Then I called a friend at a public accounting firm and got this message:

You have reached Mary Smith at XYZ Partners. I am sorry I cannot take your call right now. Most likely I am in client meetings and not able to check my voice mail immediately. However, I do check my messages around 7:30 every morning and again after work in the evening. If you have an urgent need to reach me, please contact my assistant at _____.

Once I heard that message, I knew that if I wanted to talk to Mary today, I would have to contact her secretary. But her message also made me question the urgency of my call. Since it wasn't that urgent, I left a voice mail, knowing I probably wouldn't hear back until later that day or the next morning. Another advantage of Mary's message was that it told me she was doing something important (client meetings) so I understood why she wasn't returning my call immediately.

Using Mary's basic formula, you too can construct a voice mail or answering machine announcement that tells the listener when to expect a response. First you record the obligatory identification of who you are and your regret at missing the message. Then, if you think it's necessary, give a credible rationale as to why you have more important things to do than immediately react to your phone mail. Like Mary, your work may be client meetings. Or maybe it is project meetings. Or perhaps you could use an explanation like "I'm working toward a deadline." If you travel a lot, you can say, "I am apt to be on the road right now." The key is to use an activity that (1) you do frequently, (2) sounds important, and (3) implies it can't be wrapped up in ten minutes. The rationale need not be literally true. Mary used the phrase "most likely" to allow herself some wiggle room.

It may be you can't come up with a credible rationale for your phone announcement. If not, just keep silent about the reasons why. Remember that the purpose of this announcement is to help others understand you have specific times when you review messages. It isn't to leave a detailed excuse why you're not immediately available.

Whether or not you give a reason for your unavailability, tell the caller when and how often you check your messages. If possible, consider mentioning how to get in touch with you if the call is truly urgent.

Many e-mail systems also allow you to send some sort of announcement that explains your timetable for returning e-mails. Most people use these automatic replies only when they are out of the office for several days. However, there's no reason not to use such a message all the time, especially if you feel uncomfortable about letting an e-mail languish for many hours. Simple is best when it comes to e-mail, so a message like, "Thanks for your message. I'm not on-line now, but I do check my messages at least once a day. I'll get back to you soon." acknowledges receipt of a message while telling senders when they might expect a reply. This doesn't mean that you can't check your messages more frequently. It just allows you to maintain control and to remind yourself that you are not under some vague obligation to the electronic transmission gods.

Reining In Your Pager

There is more to life than increasing its speed.
Mahatma Gandhi

Referring callers to a pager number, if you have one, can be a mixed blessing. Your callers may show self-restraint and only call your pager when appropriate. Or they may page you no matter what their need. Since pager numbers are hard to retract once given out, generally it makes sense to limit their distribution.

If you do provide others with your pager number, be sure to set people's expectations so you are not racing to find a phone each time you hear the beep. Here are some techniques from a longtime pager user:

*Whenever I give out my pager number, I try to (nicely) let
people know what is/isn't pager appropriate. I also point out
that if I am with someone, I may not be able to return the call
for a while. I must admit, however, that I've memorized the
phone numbers of a few people. If they call, I make a point to
get back to them as soon as I can.*

This telecommunications director makes sure he doesn't get
paged unnecessarily:

*My boss and my direct reports all have my pager number. I
also leave it on my phone mail message in case someone has
an urgent need to contact me. Do people ever contact me
when it's not an emergency? They may do it once, but they
never do it again.*

Managing Your Clients

*Oh, how often I wished that Thomas A. Watson had laid a
restraining hand on A. G. Bell's arm and had said to him,
"Let's not and say we did."*
Jean Mercier

If you're in a sales or customer contact position, it's particularly important to manage your clients' presumptions of your
availability. Some clients are more demanding than others are
and they never hesitate to try to reach you whatever the circumstances. Luckily, these people are the exceptions. Most
clients can understand realistic boundaries if you make them
clear. When a client knows that you reliably call back when

you say you will, he or she will be less concerned about the swiftness of your response.

One real estate agent describes his techniques this way:

> My clients have my pager number but they also understand that I don't stop in the middle of client meetings or home tours to return a page. If someone gives me a hard time about that, then I point out to him that I don't interrupt our meeting time to call someone else. This does mean that I have to be disciplined about scheduling time to return pages. I can't let myself be stuck on the road all day long without a break to make some calls.

This saleswoman has her own theory about paging:

> If a particular client pages me a lot when there really isn't any urgency, I think it is because they are testing me somehow. So I start being a lot more proactive with them, checking in every few days. And if there is a day when I know it will be hard to return their pages, I call to let them know a day or so in advance and ask if I can do anything for them while I have them on the phone. I call it "killing them with kindness" and it generally works pretty well.

Are You Sure You Want to Change?

Science finds, industry applies, man conforms.
Anonymous

Limiting the times you pick up messages, setting up screens, and setting other people's expectations are all ways that you can reestablish control over your electronic communications. But none of these methods is effective if you can't change your own behavior. Being on the receiving end of messages makes you feel important within your organization. It means that other people care enough to contact you. You are "in the loop." Ignoring messages, even for a few hours, can be more than some people can bear.

If you find yourself addicted to checking messages, try to figure out why. Is it curiosity? Is it the desire for stimulation? Are you looking for a distraction from what you are working on? I must confess, I'm an e-mail junkie. I'll postpone almost any chore, no matter how important or urgent, just to see if anyone cares about me enough to have sent a message. When I was writing this book, I had to limit myself to checking e-mail when I first sat down to work and again after lunch. Otherwise I would check every twenty minutes and never get any momentum. For a period of time I was living in Italy, which is nine time zones away from San Francisco, where most of my friends live. I would check my e-mail first thing in the morning Italian time, 11 P.M. on the West Coast, and then again at lunch, which would be 4 A.M. in California. Who, you may ask, was I expecting to write to me in the darkest hours of night? No one really, but it never hurts to hope.

So if you are like me, you may find that you don't mind checking messages frequently and you don't want to unleash yourself from every electronic tether. However, if you find that keeping up with your messages hampers your ability to accomplish your high-priority tasks at work or that they interrupt you when you're spending time on other Personal Priorities, you need to establish some limits.

This independent contractor has reached her conclusion:

Basically, I learned that I had to control the technology and not let it control me. I needed to set rules and boundaries. If not, it becomes a never-ending cycle that's hard to break. If people know you are reachable at all hours, they'll use that. In my case, it started out as "emergencies only" (which is sometimes necessary), then slowly became part of my routine (which is not good).

Who are you going to let control your limited time—you or the person transmitting the message?

Exploration Exercises

Looking in the Mirror

1. Developing an objective sense of what messages you receive will help reestablish your sense of control over your electronic devices. For a day or two, keep a log of what messages come in: who sends them, by what medium (e-mail, voice mail, pager, etc.), when they were sent, when you answered them, your rating of the urgency of that message, and your best guess how urgent the sender thought the message was. It is also useful to determine whether or not any action was required on your part. (See the sample on page 148.) Once you have your log, ask yourself the following questions:
   - How many of your messages were important? How many were time critical? To you? To the sender?
   - How many of your messages were from someone who is important to you?

- How many of your messages were related to your Personal Priorities?
- How many times during the day did you interrupt what you were doing to respond to a message? Were those interruptions time well spent?

2. Do you respond to messages quickly because it's required for your job or is it a result of your desire to meet other people's expectations? Imagine that you only picked up your messages every four hours. What would be the repercussions on your work life? On your home life? Can you think of a way that only your truly important messages would interrupt your day and the rest would wait until you were ready to pick them up?

Sample Message Log

MESSAGE SENT BY	E-MAIL, PHONE MAIL, OR PAGER	TIME IT WAS SENT	TIME I GOT BACK TO THEM	MY SENSE OF THE MESSAGE'S URGENCY	SENDER'S SENSE OF URGENCY	COMMENTS
Lisa	e-mail	Monday 9 AM	Monday 2 PM	Mild	Mild	No big deal
My boss	e-mail	Monday 10 AM	Monday 2 PM	Mild	Important	No big deal
My son	pager	Monday 3:30 PM	Monday 3:35 PM	Mild	Important	Have to clarify rules of paging me at work

Commute Questions

(These questions are for you to ponder when you are commuting, waiting in line, etc. Think of them as directed daydreams.)

On your way home, ask yourself if there is anyone you really want to talk to this evening. If the answer is yes, why not give them a call? If the answer is no, unplug your phone and give yourself an uninterrupted evening. Remember, Miss Manners says this is perfectly acceptable behavior.

Action Steps

Incorporate into your voice mail, e-mail, or answering machine a message that sets the expectations of the caller/sender that: (1) you only pick up messages at the end of the day (or every four hours or whatever works for you), and (2) if it is an emergency, how they can reach you. Now, try to live by that discipline and restrain yourself from checking for messages too frequently. Keep it up for at least three to four days and see how it gives you a new sense of control.

> To me, having a balanced life means a complete break from work at home—not running to the phone to leave just one more phone mail or to the computer at 4 A.M. to run off a series of e-mails. It's having some real downtime to thumb through a catalog or play dominoes.
>
> A mother of three, corporate vice president, and part-time faculty member at an MBA program

Granting Yourself the Gift of Time

GIVING WHERE IT COUNTS

A friend and I are having a cup of coffee at a little neighborhood restaurant. Our bill is less than $2, but my friend leaves the waitress a dollar bill as a tip. The service has been nothing special, so I ask her why she tipped so much.

"There isn't a lot of difference between a regular tip and what I gave her. It means very little to me. But to that waitress, a nice tip might be important and I know it will make her feel good. So why shouldn't I put my money where it can make a difference?"

Where are you spending your time? Where it is proscribed, or where it might be really important?

What is having a balanced life worth to you? If you could write a check and be guaranteed a greater sense of control and happiness, how big a check would you write? One day's pay? A week's pay? More? What if I told you that you could have a more balanced life and all it would take would be an hour or two a week? Would you accept that bargain?

If your answer is yes, then there's a small miracle waiting for you. Once you carve away one or two hours a week from your normal routine and devote those hours to what is truly important to you, you will feel more in control. You will have added more balance to your existence. That such a small change makes your life so much better is a blessing and a mystery.

Part of the secret of this unexpected phenomenon is explained by "the relative value of an extra hour" mentioned in Chapter 5. When ten or so hours of your day are devoted to work and only a few hours a day are spent nurturing your home life, you can take an hour from work, and then use that hour to greatly expand the time for your other Personal Priorities. But the truth is, you don't even have to take an hour from every workday. By spending just one or two hours a week on something meaningful, you are demonstrating that you can wrench control of your time from your job and return it to the person who truly appreciates it: you.

If You Give Yourself an Hour . . .

We carry with us the wonders we seek without us.

Sir Thomas Browne

For some of us, squeezing an hour or two away from work every week seems like an unattainable goal. Yet this hour could turn out to be the most memorable hour of your week. Listen to this manager's story about her "ice cream socials":

A few months ago, I decided to change my schedule on Tuesdays. I now start work earlier in the morning and I leave the office at 4, which is a whole lot earlier than I used to. I pick my kids up from after-school care, but instead of going home, we go for an ice cream. We sit around one of those tiny sticky tables and I get to hear about what happened at school that day. It seems like a small thing, but on normal evenings, we just don't have the time to talk. Lots of times I feel guilty about being a full-time working mom. These ice cream socials really help me feel connected to my kids.

This woman was practicing an exercise I call "the gift of time." It involves taking an hour or two from your typically overscheduled week and spending it on one of your Personal Priorities. You give this time to yourself as a present.

Giving yourself the gift of time is a very simple exercise, one that you can begin right now. Remind yourself of what your Personal Priorities are. Now take a moment and think about what you would like to do related to one of those Priorities that would only take an hour or two. Watch the sunset with someone you love? Go for a jog along a wooded path? Have lunch in a café with a friend? Visit an avant-garde art gallery? Spend an hour in a garden with your child? Close your eyes, take a deep breath, and imagine what it would be like. Create the image for yourself in as much detail as you can: where you are, who you are with, what you see, what you hear, how you feel. Even this little imagination break is pleasant, isn't it?

Now it's time to schedule the real thing. Put down this book, get your calendar, pick up the phone, and start to make the arrangements.

You have just run into the hard part. While looking at your calendar, there may seem to be no time. While an hour to do what you love sounds appealing, there is no empty space to put it in.

On a rational level, you know that finding time for yourself should not be an onerous task. After all, you're the one who decided what you wanted to do. It'll be wonderful to nurture one of your Personal Priorities. Is work really that important? Go ahead and take the hour, if for no other reason than to see what happens.

What the Gift of Time Can Do

For lack of attention a thousand forms of loveliness elude us
every day.
Evelyn Underhill

In my workshops, I ask people to take the gift of time exercise and then report back to the group what their experiences were like. What people choose varies tremendously—from getting a massage to taking a hang-gliding lesson to going out on a date with their spouse. For each person, however, this small gift of time is surprisingly precious, for they are starting the process of restoring their souls.

Here are some examples, the first from a man who lives in Northern California:

I live about one mile from the beach and ever since we moved there, I told myself I should go walk on the beach some evening after work. So the evening after the workshop, I just did it. I drove down there, parked, and walked along the water for a while. Then I sat on a log and watched the sunset. It was beautiful. When I got home later that evening, I was able to bring the serenity of that experience

with me. My wife was so impressed, she encouraged me to
stop by the beach every day.

This man discovered a very simple pleasure for himself, one that literally has been waiting for him at his own back door. All he had to do was break his normal routine to allow himself the gift of some time.

Surprisingly, our routines sometimes work against our ability to find balance. As we rush unconsciously from desk to home and back again, we lose sight of potential opportunities. Bursting free from our normal patterns, whether to visit a beach or call an old friend, rewards us with moments we can savor for days.

Another gift of time story comes from a project analyst who wanted to see more of the world:

This may sound strange, but I decided to take French lessons.
I really like to travel but since I started this job, I can't seem
to take the time to go anywhere. By signing up for language
lessons, I feel I am making a major commitment to myself.
Even driving to and from my lessons makes me happy as I
daydream of nibbling croissants at a sidewalk café with church
bells tolling in the distance.

Many of us are in work situations where our dreams of adventure, creativity, or travel seem 10,000 miles away. But in reality very little is needed to keep our dreams vibrant. Taking a language class, spending an hour at an art studio, or attending a lecture series can pump nourishment into our dreams and into our souls.

Sneaking In a Gift of Time

Do what you can, with what you have, where you are.
Theodore Roosevelt

Taking advantage of the gift of time doesn't always have to be planned. Generally in any typical week, something in your schedule doesn't happen as anticipated. Meetings are canceled, appointments are late, or travel plans get delayed. Instead of railing against these uncontrolled events, take advantage of the time and use them for your Personal Priorities like this sales representative did:

> *I went to an appointment with a client, only to discover she was running late and I had to wait half an hour. I asked for access to a phone, but instead of doing only work-related calls, I first called some friends and invited them to come over for a potluck dinner that weekend. It's funny how well it worked out. On my commute in, I had been wondering when I would get a chance to see my friends ("Having close friends" is one of my Personal Priorities), and that free half hour gave me the chance to do something about it.*

Being conscious of what you want from your life helps you take advantage of opportunities as they speed past. If this sales rep hadn't been thinking of his Personal Priorities, he might have sat in a waiting room reading outdated magazines instead of arranging a dinner with friends. But because he knew what he wanted from his life, he was able to make it happen.

Another woman keeps herself prepared for unexpected gifts of time:

> When I start feeling guilty about not writing to my out-of-town friends but don't have time to do anything about it, I pull out an envelope and take a minute to address and stamp it. Then I carry the envelope around with me. More times than not, within a few days I have fifteen or twenty minutes with nothing to do, so I jot a friend a letter, stick it in the waiting envelope, and drop it in the mail. It really helps me keep in touch with friends I rarely see.

Taking Control of Your Days

First say to yourself what you would be, and then do
what you have to do.
Epictetus

Of course, nuggets of time don't always fall into your lap. Sometimes you have to pry yourself away from work for a gift of time. Generally the results are well worth it, as demonstrated by this story from a young working mother with a 5-year-old daughter:

> I decided to give myself the gift of time and go visit my daughter's kindergarten class. It was extremely hard for me to leave work in the middle of the day. It is a very busy time for us at the office. But I decided I really wanted to do it, so I made myself go. Her class was having their Valentine party. It was fun to see my daughter so excited and happy.

*And she was absolutely thrilled to have me there. You see,
this was the first time I had ever visited her class, even
though she had been in kindergarten for almost six months.
Without the gift of time, I would have missed that chapter
of her life completely.*

I asked this mom if she had missed anything important at
work in order to go to her daughter's party. She hadn't. The
truth is, few important moments in your life take place at
work. In fact, *The Wall Street Journal* recently reported that
many high-level executives regret they didn't spend more time
with their families as they clambered up the career ladder. To
paraphrase their comments, "I remember to this day what play
or performance or soccer game I missed. I just can't remember
what was so important that it took me away."

Why didn't those powerful executives seize control of their
calendars and make time for what was important? Obviously
there must have been some pressing engagement, although
not one so important that they remember it now. Luckily
there is no need for you to repeat their mistakes because you
know two things those executives probably did not.

First, you have a very clear sense of your Personal Priorities.
This knowledge gives you the inner fortitude to modify your
schedule, even if it goes against a workaholic culture. Second,
you know how to use timesaving techniques so you can create
the time for your Personal Priorities and not shortchange your
work commitments. So armed with this knowledge, it should
be relatively easy to give yourself the gift of time. And not just
for the next week, but for every week to come.

Another thing to remember is that a gift of time can be a
gift to others as well as yourself, as this person discovered:

For my gift of time, I had coffee with my mother. It's not that we never see each other. In fact, she takes care of my kids while I work. But most of our conversations are about the kids, who's not feeling well, how my son is doing with his homework, that kind of stuff. So one afternoon, she and I just went out together and had a wonderful chat. I loved it, and even better, so did she. She still tells me how much she enjoyed that time with me.

Living Life's Moments

Life is a succession of moments. To live each one is to succeed.
Corita Kent

If you still find that you're having difficulty scheduling an hour as a gift for yourself, then go back to the prior chapters and remind yourself of the timesaving techniques we discussed. Examine all the entries on your calendar. Are you sure there aren't at least some that could be shortened or wiped away through the power of prioritizing, delegating, simplifying, setting time limits, procrastinating, or eliminating?

If that approach doesn't create openings in your calendar, then maybe you're exaggerating the importance of all those hours at work. It's rather embarrassing to admit to ourselves, but most of us could take an hour off from our jobs next week and no one would miss us. Realistically, when you think about what is scheduled for next week, how much of it is really going to matter six months from now? When I ask this question of people who attend my workshops, nearly all look down at their shoe tops and give sheepish little laughs. The truth is, most of what we work so hard on in any given day has minimal importance six months from now. Or even one month from now. Some things we work on may never have any importance.

Yet giving yourself a gift of time does have importance. It is one of the steps you must take in order to reclaim your authentic self. It is an acknowledgment that you have Personal Priorities that transcend the workplace. And most importantly, taking a gift of time not only shows you have other priorities, but that you're willing to act on them. For without action, the best intentions are indistinguishable from the worst.

This story of a hard-driving businessman and father is the flip side of the story told by the kindergartner's mom:

> I always planned to spend at least one day a school year with my son's class, either helping in the classroom or going on a field trip. One day a year didn't sound like a big commitment, but somehow there was always a conflict and I would only make it every other year, if that. Finally, I decided to cut down on my work hours and told my son, who was now in the sixth grade, that I planned to spend a lot of time in his classroom this year. To my horror, he almost started crying. "Please, don't, Daddy," he said. "I can't tell you why, I just don't want you there." Bewildered, I talked to his teacher about it. She explained to me that by the sixth grade, some students no longer are comfortable having their parents come to the classroom. They are starting to turn into adolescents. Sadly disappointed, I realized that an opportunity had passed me by. There were only six years during which I could visit my son's class, and I was so busy, I missed most of them.

Postponing what is important to you until the next year is a high-risk approach. This father deluded himself into thinking his son would always welcome him into his life. Yet the boy entered adolescence earlier than the dad had expected. He'd simply waited too long. Sometimes postponement is inevitable, but it is always precarious. Can you look into the future and be assured that what might be difficult today won't be impossible tomorrow?

Getting Beyond Excuses

The world is full of wonders and miracles but man takes his little
hand and covers his eyes and sees nothing.
Israel Baal Shem

Postponement is just one of many justifications for not giving yourself the gift of time. Think about your own excuses. Do they reflect your unwillingness to step over the unseen boundaries of a workaholic culture? Do you need some more self-discipline to alter your personal patterns? Are you somehow reluctant to change? Here are some of the rationalizations I hear from people who don't honor their Personal Priorities enough to give themselves the gift of time:

Rationalization: *"I am getting paid for work. I can't take time for myself when there's still work to be done."*

My response: What are you being paid to do? Working "until the work is done" is a vague and nonbinding expectation, especially since in today's world the work is never done. Think of your contract with your employer as a rental agreement. Your employer has the right to certain (but not all) aspects of you for a certain (but not unlimited) amount of time. No matter where you work, they can't be paying you enough to claim every hour of your time. No paycheck is so hefty that it can compensate for abandoning all joy in your life. If you have been working more than 40 hours a week without a direct increase in salary, you have been gifting that time to your employer. It's now time to be a bit less generous and reclaim at least one or two of those hours for yourself.

A financial analyst in a busy department managed to take her gift of time this way:

> A couple days ahead of time, I started telling everyone that I had to leave early on Friday. I didn't give an excuse but I was very clear about it. Then when Friday came, I reminded everyone again that I was going to be leaving early. It turns out it was a nonevent. After a while, I realized I was talking so much about it so I could convince myself it was all right. No one else seemed to care.

Rationalization: *"Other people are counting on me to pull my weight. I can't let my team down."*

My response: Team pressure, or peer pressure, is always a potent force in shaping the behavior of individuals. Teams have a powerful motivation to maintain group norms and disallow individual preferences. Sometimes they choose those norms because they know of no other way. By modeling a balanced life to your peers, you can show them how various time-saving techniques help create more time for personal renewal. Odds are, there are members of your group who are as hungry for a balanced life as you are, and would be delighted to have you lead the way.

An individual who attended a Balanced Life workshop told this story:

> I work in an office with only six other people so it was very hard for me to leave early. In fact, some of my co-workers

were quite irritated with me. But I was back on the job early the next morning, feeling more charged and energetic than I had in weeks. When I told them about my gift of time and how much I enjoyed it, I could tell that many of them were envious. When I see what a positive benefit it has on my attitude and my work, I encourage everyone to take some time for him- or herself, especially if things are really busy.

Rationalization: *"I know I should do this. It's just that this is a busy time. I've put off spending time on myself for so long, one more week won't matter."*

My response: Sometimes delay is inevitable. The question is: how is the next week going to be different from this one? If it truly is less busy, you're very lucky. Schedule your gift of time now so you'll be sure to do it next week. But if next week is as busy as this one is, or you keep rescheduling your gift of time into the future, you have to deal with the fact that your actions don't jibe with your values. You said your Personal Priorities are important, so why aren't you honoring them?

If you are in the midst of a very busy time, why not use a gift of time as a reward for hitting some milestone in a project, like this designer did:

Looking at my schedule over the next few weeks, I didn't think I could ever give myself the gift of time. But then I decided that if I worked really efficiently and finished a particularly challenging piece of the project by Wednesday, I would reward myself with a gift of time. It was funny, but the promise of that time really motivated me and I was done by Wednesday. So I gave myself the gift of time and had a great evening. It was the perfect reward for all my hard work.

Rationalization: *"I never got the time to get myself organized to make it happen." "We couldn't find a baby-sitter." "I really wanted to see this concert but it was sold out and by that time it was too late to do anything else."*

My response: Building a balanced life requires change. You have to be willing to modify how you spend your time. Sometimes the idea of making changes intimidates people. When this happens, the excuses start. Relatively small barriers swell into insurmountable obstacles. As you build your self-awareness, you'll be able to recognize this behavior in yourself.

Sometimes, conquering one small barrier can propel you into the gift of time habit as it did for this overworked professional:

I kept telling my husband that we should go out once a week to get away from the house and the chores and everything, but I never seemed to get organized. Finally, I asked one of the neighborhood teenagers to baby-sit for us every Thursday night. That was all we needed to get going. Because we know she's coming, we now have a date every Thursday, even if it's only to share a pizza at the mall.

Replenish and Restore

Each day provides its own gifts.
Ruth Freedom

The final irony facing people who don't give themselves the gift of time is that taking that time can actually enhance your work life. No employer striving for success wants an organization filled with dead-eyed employees grinding billions of bits of useless information through their PCs. The most valued employees today are those who can demonstrate creative problem solving, flexibility, and the ability to get along with others. It is difficult, if not impossible, to manifest those qualities if your soul is deprived of the nourishment it requires. How do you go about replenishing your soul? Simply give yourself an hour to expand your focus beyond the office walls. By investing time in whatever is important to you, you will be able to rekindle a joy and enthusiasm that will automatically spill over and benefit your work life as well.

Exploration Exercise

Looking in the Mirror

Visualization is a technique used to help you get what you want from your life. For example, athletes use visualization to picture taking the perfect swing or making the perfect shot. You can also use this technique to create for yourself a perfect gift of time.

This visualization technique is most effective if you can listen to the instructions while you are relaxed with your eyes closed. If you can't find someone to read it to you, read it into a cassette recorder and play it back for yourself. Or listen to a modification of it on my Web site: www.comingupforair.com. Less desirable but still workable is to read it to yourself, but close your eyes and do the suggested visualization between paragraphs.

GIVING YOURSELF THE GIFT OF TIME

Sit comfortably in your chair. Have both feet on the floor and your arms by your side. Close your eyes. Take three deep breaths, very slowly, exhaling completely after each breath.

Now let your breath continue, a little slower and deeper than usual. Imagine you are leaving your workplace for the day. It is not particularly late; in fact, some of your colleagues are still there. You are very comfortable about leaving, however, for today is the day you have promised yourself the gift of time.

You walk down the hall and outside into the light. But instead of being outside of your workplace, you are already where you had planned to be for your gift of time. You notice that the light is brighter and the colors are clearer than usual—you are going to have a wonderful time.

Now visualize where you are and what you are doing for your gift of time. Maybe you are in a coffee shop or restaurant, sitting opposite someone you really care about. You hear the two of you laughing together. Maybe you are seated on the floor of your living room with your child on your lap. You can smell her freshly washed hair. Maybe you are walking with your dog along a beach, inhaling the briny air and feeling the rough sand under your bare feet.

Take a moment, and fill out the picture you have made for yourself. Imagine as many details as you can. What do you see? What are you hearing? Are there any particularly pleasant smells or sensations?

After you have a clear picture, take another series of slow deep breaths. Now open your eyes. This is the end of your visualization.

Now imagine you were given one to two free hours next week. The only criterion is that you have to use those hours in a way that makes you feel you have a more balanced life. Next, write down the answers to the following questions (you might first want to review your Personal Priorities):

- What would you do? How would doing this activity make you feel better?
- Is there any benefit to you in maintaining the status quo and not giving yourself the gift of time?

Commute Questions

(*These questions are for you to ponder when you are commuting, waiting in line, etc. Think of them as directed daydreams.*)

- Imagine other gifts of time that you would like to take. Try to create at least one for each of your Personal Priorities. They should be for at least one hour, but can be longer.
- (*If you find it difficult to commit yourself to taking off an hour for a gift of time, use this exercise on the way home.*) Review your workday in your head, hour by hour. How many of those hours were spent on work that is going to matter one month, three months, or six months from now? Was there an hour in the day just past that could have been spent on something that was more important to you?

Action Step

What steps could you take in the next twenty-four hours that would commit you to taking a gift of time and using it as you described earlier? Go ahead and take those steps and schedule your gift of time for sometime in the next seven days.

> To me, having a balanced life means having the freedom to do what I want when I want. It's taking the time to stop and smell the roses, to look at the sky and stare at the stars and the moon, and to take my children to a museum in the middle of the week.
>
> **A 34-year-old manager and father of four**

Part 3:

SPECIAL CIRCUMSTANCES,
SPECIAL RESPONSES

Let the beauty we love

be what we do.

There are hundreds of ways to kneel

and kiss the ground.

Jelaluddin Rumi

Balancing with Babies and Other Children

THE BOY AND THE COOKIES

A little boy sneaks into the kitchen and sees a large jar of cookies on the counter. He sticks his hand in and grabs as many as he can. But when he tries to pull his hand out, he can't; the mouth of the jar is too narrow.

Instead of dropping some of the cookies back into the jar, he becomes frustrated and starts crying until his mother comes in.

*Do you ever get stymied when trying to grasp too many
good things at the same time?*

As a working parent and particularly a working mother, balance stops being an option and starts becoming a necessity. Once children enter your life, success in your career can no longer be your exclusive goal. It can be one of your goals and in fact, it is still an obtainable goal. But you can no longer be single-minded. As is frequently quoted in today's women's circles, "You can have it all, just not all at the same time."

While balance is an issue with almost everyone in this workaholic world, parents feel particular pressure. For having children gives your home life not only a face and a voice but also a vulnerable personality. When you are single and you neglect your home life, you are damaging only yourself. If you are married and work too much, your spouse may not like it, but as an adult, he or she has options on how to remedy that situation. Children, on the other hand, are very restricted in how they can counter parents who work too much. Children have many needs, and some of these only a parent can fulfill. And parents want to be there to take care of their children's needs. But too often, looming up between the parent and the child is the Job.

The Woes of the Working Parent

At work, you think of the children you've left at home. At home, you think of the work you've left unfinished. Such a struggle is unleashed within yourself, your heart is rent.
Golda Meir

When I asked some of the parents in my Balanced Life class if they would ever take a job that paid less but allowed more time for a home life, this was a typical reply:

> I wish I could take a job that allowed me to spend more time on my home life but we can't afford it. I'm missing my children and missing their growing-up years (three girls ages 12, 9, and 1). The pain is so real, I can feel it.

Even parents who don't necessarily want to work fewer hours feel conflicted as they try to meet the simultaneous obligations of work and home. As if juggling commitments wasn't challenge enough, our culture also manages to make mothers, although rarely fathers, feel guilty about working.

During the Clinton/Lewinsky episode, I read a *New York Times* editorial that attributed America's moral decline to the fact that today's children aren't getting enough time and attention from their parents. The solution? Women should stop working and stay home. There was no mention of the father staying home. To this writer's mind, the man's career track should be undisturbed. This article infuriated me *and* made me feel vaguely guilty, which infuriated me even more. Once I cooled down, I remembered the passage on guilt in Chapter 3 and realized this writer doesn't have the right to expect anything from me, or for that matter, from any working mother.

The people that do have a right to expect something from us are our children. It's critical for parents to stay conscious of the time and relationship compromises we make between our children and our work. Think about those trade-offs carefully, discuss them with your partner if you have one, and use your best judgment. Then build enough structure and safeguards into your life so you can feel good about your performance as a worker and as a parent.

Unfortunately, you'll probably find little societal or corporate assistance available to you in your efforts to combine work and parenting. Let's face it—your boss couldn't care less about your daughter's struggles with the multiplication tables or your son's colic. Your co-workers resent your leaving early to attend a piano recital. Your clients are irritated when you're unavailable because of a school field trip. You spend half your day surrounded by people who care nothing about your family or the love you feel for your children. And when you go home, you'll find that your children care nothing about your boss and co-workers or the devotion you may feel for your job. Your dilemma is how to reconcile those two sides of your life without neglecting either or driving yourself crazy.

One employed mother decided to adopt a "don't ask, don't tell" approach at her job and avoided talking about her family:

> I finally decided that it wasn't worth sharing what was going on with my family with the people at work. There weren't any overt signs of disapproval, but I sensed that whenever something wasn't perfect in my work, they would attribute it to my split priorities as a working mother. It's true—because of my kids, I have to leave right on time. So it became easier to not make a big deal of my family responsibilities but to just focus on getting my work done.

Once again, we find that building a balanced life can be a lonely undertaking. For many working parents, the mantra of "focus on work at work, focus on home at home" helps get them through their week. And one of the requirements of being able to focus on work at work is to be assured of good child care.

The Never-Ending Search for Good Child Care

Having a baby . . . brought home to me with a real force the hopelessly unbalanced nature of a society which is organized solely for the needs of people without responsibility for children.
Angela Phillips

There is nothing harder than finding affordable, reliable, and convenient child care. Even families in which one of the parents chooses to stay home with the children can have difficulties. The rest of us contend with decade-long struggles. We all know it's critical to get the best child care we can afford, particularly for the first years. From birth to about 4 years old, the more stimulation and attention a child gets, the better he or she scores on cognitive and language tests. This nurturing doesn't have to come from a parent, but it does have to come from a responsible adult. This means you have to identify exceptionally good child-care situations. Shortchanging your child during this period is not a trade-off you want to make.

Economically and emotionally, finding superb child care and maintaining it for years can be extremely draining. You find the perfect day-care center and the rates are higher than you can afford. Your mother was going to take care of the children but now her health is failing. Your flawless nanny gets pregnant with her own baby. Or you find a situation that works well but perversely, it lasts only a few months. This family went through two different child-care situations in less than a year and their experience is not unusual:

Our first experience with child care was after my son was 8 months old. We chose to have in-home care for him because both my wife and I wanted to maintain professional careers. Our plans were disrupted when our in-home care provider had to take care of an adult daughter who was seriously injured. We then decided to use a professional day-care center. Our son adapted well to having other children around and was very happy when he was there. But when he was 15 months, he suddenly had to be taken to the hospital. My wife and I were notified, but we were both at least an hour away. After that, we knew we had to find yet another alternative.

Sometimes, even when you have good child care, the responsibilities of your job overflow into your home life and prevent you from doing what is right for your family, as described by this mother and manager:

I had just started a new job and was supervising a group of people I didn't know very well. There were a lot of personnel issues within the group and that was very draining for me emotionally. When I got home, I wanted to see my children, but I really didn't want to talk to the woman who was taking care of them. I saw it as dealing with just one more employee, one more set of problems. Later, I realized how that perspective was a big mistake. She resented the fact that I was avoiding her, and the communication between us got even worse. It was a bad situation for her, for me, and of course, for my children.

Know What's Going On with Your Child's Caretaker

Before I got married I had six theories about bringing up children; now I have six children, and no theories.
Lord Rochester

Looking back at my own child-care situations, I shudder at some of the mistakes I made. My husband and I both held office jobs and had no relatives in town. Therefore we depended on day-care centers, preschools, and various nannies and baby-sitters. When my son was in day care, the center started out strong, but later, staff turnover had become rampant. My normal routine had been to drop my son off at the day-care center, run off to work, and then race back to pick him up seconds before the late fees began. Because I was so focused at work, it was months before I realized I didn't recognize most of the caretakers' faces. And I wondered why my son had acted so withdrawn lately!

That incident should have taught me there was a price to pay when I focused too heavily on my work instead of my child's care. But being a slow learner at times, I next hired a nanny I knew was only adequate. I didn't want to risk missing days or even weeks of work while I tried to find someone else, and I thought she would work out. She didn't, and my son had to endure another child-care change.

By the time our second child was born, a little girl, I was either better trained or luckier, and we didn't have as many child-care issues. But she did not escape unscathed either. One summer, she cried at camp every day for weeks before I knew there was a problem. There hadn't been good communications among me, my daughter's camp counselor, and the baby-sitter who picked her up. Luckily, these various incidents were the exception, scattered through years of wonderful care, but they always remind me of just how hard it is to find good caretakers for my children. And how important it is for me to stay on top of the situation.

Whether as a society we are satisfied with the available child-care options we have or not, few of us live the 1950s model of the working dad and stay-at-home mother: 68% of mothers with children under 18 work outside the home, and nearly half of these mothers contribute more than half of the household income. Only six thousand companies in America offer on-site day care. So what is there to do? The only option is to make your own situation as good as you can for yourself and your children. Stay clear on your priorities, keep a close eye on your child-care provider, and don't let your job swallow all your time.

Deciding to Work Part Time

It does not matter how slowly you go, so long as you do not stop.
Confucius

There may be times when you need to step off the career track and work part time for the benefit of your children. Parents decide to take a part-time job for a wide range of reasons. They may be responding to an intuitive sense that they should spend less time at work and more time with their child. Or it may be a more serious situation, like a child with behavioral problems or the loss of a full-time job. Rarely is it an easy decision, for the monetary and career trade-offs seem enormous.

This man talks about the price he paid to work part time:

It was a big financial decision to starting working part time. My boss said I could no longer supervise people, so I had to take a demotion as well as the cut in pay because of shorter hours. I ended up earning only about 60% of what I was getting before. I was willing to make that trade-off in order to have more time with my kids, but it wasn't easy.

Or as this administrator succinctly describes her part-time experience:

I was very, very happy but very, very poor. I think my children and I benefited by my spending more time at home, but it definitely put my career on hold.

For the highly or even moderately ambitious, the idea of working part time seems like the destruction of a bright career.

These fears can fade, however, when you realize it is not a life-time commitment. In fact, your part-time years may represent only a small phase of your working life. If you believe you create a career over four decades, working half time for a few years is only a fractional decrease. Or since many people create three or even four careers for themselves, consider years on a slower track as an opportunity to refresh yourself and reexamine what you want from your job. If you are competent in your field, some company will be eager to have you return to full-time work. They may even dangle alluring salaries or sign-on bonuses in front of you to entice you back. And you might surprise yourself and not want to go back any more than this part-timer does:

> I started working half time when my first child was born and kept it up through the birth of my second. All this time, it has been in my boss's mind that I will return to full time once my youngest goes to kindergarten. Every now and then he mentions it to me, eager to have me back again on a full-time basis. But frankly, that's not what I want. I am so happy now, I just want to work part time for the rest of my life.

Working part time may stall your career for a while, but reentering the workplace on a full-time basis is not necessarily difficult. Odds are, your part-time years will rarely be an issue. With the amount of turnover and restructuring taking place in most American organizations, there is no one left to keep track of who worked how many hours in a given year. When my son was a toddler, I worked four days a week for over two years. Several years later, my husband worked three-quarter time for a period of time. We both picked up our careers where we left off. I doubt if anyone at either firm remembers or cares about the time we took off. But our children certainly bene-fited from the extra time we could spend with them.

The Part-Time Trade-Offs

Do what you feel in your heart to be right for you will be criticized anyway. You will be damned if you do, and damned if you don't.
Eleanor Roosevelt

If you decide to work part time, understand the trade-offs you're making so resentment doesn't taint your attitude toward your job. Many people find that they work nearly full-time hours in exchange for part-time pay and the opportunity to have one or two days at home during the week. While working part time doesn't end your career, it doesn't necessarily advance it either. Most firms reserve promotions, significant pay raises, and hefty bonuses for full-time workers. Sometimes benefits are reduced or even eliminated.

In addition to a lower salary, you might also find that many of the other fulfilling aspects of work lessen or even disappear when you work part time. You might feel less involved in your workplace. You might not get as many opportunities to grapple with challenging issues, and you'll long for the pride you felt from being trusted with greater responsibilities. Socially, you may be a step removed as well. You'll miss some of the get-togethers, events, and juicy gossip that serve as the interpersonal glue in organizations. If you work in an office setting, you may even find that your physical space is downgraded because full-time workers get first dibs on the best cubicle or office locations. Your self-image can be bruised as well, as this analyst described:

*I was surprised by the blow my self-esteem took when I
became a part-timer. I have also seen myself as a "player,"
someone who made major contributions at the job. Suddenly,
I feel I'm on the sidelines. I'm not invited to all the meetings.
I see my peers advance their careers ahead of me. Frankly, it's
been hard to take.*

So why would you choose to work part time? You do it
because one or more of your Personal Priorities involves your
family. Deciding that you'd prefer to invest your time and
energy in your family can make perfect sense. Creating balance in your life frequently means choosing between two very
desirable options. Once you take the time to be conscious of
the choices you're making, you'll make the decision that is
right for you.

Making the Most of the Time You Have

*The most important thing she'd learned over the years was that
there was no way to be a perfect mother and a million ways
to be a good one.*
Jill Churchill

Whether you work 20-hour weeks or 50-hour weeks, you need
to make a conscious decision about how you spend your non-
working hours with your children. Any particular time with
your child can be joyful or it can be irritating and disappointing. As a working parent with limited hours, you want to maximize the good times and minimize the bad. And somehow you
need to convince your children to cooperate with you in

achieving that. But children have their own internal clocks, calendars, and scorecards, so sometimes what we expect is not what we get.

Here is the story of a marketing manager returning home after being away for several days on business:

I had been on a particularly grueling business trip. Because I wanted to minimize how long I was away, each day was packed. I finally got home early one evening, dropped my briefcase and garment bag in the entry hall, and called to my kids. Instead of ecstatic bodies racing to throw their arms around me, I heard only muffled hellos from the TV room. I went to the kitchen where my husband was boiling water for spaghetti. At least he kissed me, but I felt like an unexpected guest in my own home.

Sometimes when a parent is away from home a lot, the family copes by filling in the gaps behind her. If your job keeps you from being a regular attendee in your family's life, you may find that you have to shove your way back in. The most effective way to do this is to establish some structured commitments or traditions that you participate in and your kids can rely on. It's best if these are made on a weekly basis. A week may be a long time on a child's calendar, but it's easy for them to grasp that every Wednesday is mom-and-dad-are-home-for-pizza night.

Many working parents have told me how they maintain contact with their families through weekly events. These times become sacred, as a gathering of loved ones in the midst of a too-busy world. Even the busiest travel schedule can be designed to preserve time with your children, as shown by this executive:

Even though I traveled all over the country for my job, I made sure I was home to have dinner with my wife and my girls on Friday nights. We have three daughters and they would take turns choosing the restaurant. One daughter always chose the same place; another was an adventurer and took us to some places I would never eat at again. My daughters are grown now, but we all remember those dinners as time we could talk about our week, share weekend plans, but most important, just be together as a family.

This public relations specialist created a different kind of Friday tradition:

I set up my hours so I work a shorter day on Fridays just so I can take my kids to school and pick them up again. It has become a very special time for them—in the morning we buy doughnuts and in the evening we stop at the convenience store and buy Slurpees. (I know it's a lot of junk food but I don't let that bother me.) It seems like a pretty small thing to me, but my children look forward to it all week. I've told my boss I won't travel on Fridays anymore—that day is reserved for my kids and me.

Other families made Sundays their special day, as in the following story:

I made a rule that I was not going to drive on Sundays anymore. As a single working mom with three kids, I found that I spent all my week either at the job or in a car. Most Sundays we just hang around the house, reading or being out in the garden. If one of my children really wants to do something, they have to arrange the transportation. Or the older one takes the bus. I found that by giving the chauffeur—me—the day off, our family took a much needed break from running around so much. With less to do, we could just be us.

My family and I created our own approach. It bugged me that my kids were spending so much time watching television, so I made a new rule—no TV or video games on Sunday. (I don't watch much TV myself and certainly don't play video games, so it's easy for me to make these kinds of rules.) What I didn't realize was that this decision made my husband and me interact with our children more. Our daughter, who wasn't old enough to read when we first made this rule, was particularly needy. So we found a complete deck of cards, dragged out the *Candyland* board, and started playing various games together. If the TV set were on, she would be watching it and, secretly I would be content because I could catch up on my chores. The "Sunday is no-TV day" rule turned out to be a good thing for all of us.

Make a Date and Keep It

These are magic years . . . and therefore magic days . . . and therefore magic moments.
Anonymous

Some parents set up weekly dates with their children to be sure to spend some one-on-one time together. This accountant writes,

I have three sons and a full-time job so my ability to have any one-on-one time with any of them is very limited. So I make

a date with one of them each weekend when we spend a couple hours doing what they want. My youngest is easy—he always wants to go to McDonald's for lunch. With my older boys, I end up in more varied activities, like indoor rock climbing, tossing a Frisbee in the park, or playing video games at the mall. Even if I'm not wild about the activity itself, the time we spend together is always worthwhile.

An established date with your children accumulates power through its regularity and reliability. It doesn't take many broken promises or unfulfilled commitments for children to learn that they're not among the most important priorities in your life. If you say you're going to be home for dinner Thursday night, don't be late. If you tell your daughter you'll take her to the mall on Saturday, do it. Imagine you had an appointment with your boss or your boss's boss. Would you ever break it or be late? Probably not. If your children are important to you, don't they deserve the same respect?

While you're making sure you spend weekly time with your children, don't forget to spend quality time with your spouse as well. Most couples with children have already learned the value of a "date night" where just the two of them go off and have dinner, go to a movie, or do the other activities they enjoyed before the babies arrived. These evenings give you and your mate a chance to reconnect emotionally, intellectually, and maybe even physically. Balancing both children and a job is draining. Quiet time with your partner helps revive your soul.

The Joy of Spontaneous Time

The only way to live is to accept each minute as an unrepeatable
miracle, which is exactly what it is—a miracle and unrepeatable.
Margaret Storm Jameson

Structured time and reliable commitments all tell your child
that he or she matters to you. But frequently, the most joyous
moments of parenthood come unexpectedly. As a working
mom or dad, how do you get your share of those glorious yet
unplanned moments?

A first step is to free yourself from the tyranny of the clock.
Once you're home, take off your watch, leave it on the bureau,
and adopt a more flexible attitude toward time. If dinner is fifteen minutes late or if baths are cut short, it's nothing to fuss
about. Instead of striving to control every moment, let events
unfold unexpectedly around you. At very unpredictable intervals, your child covets your attention. Sometimes the reason is
a great one, like two gold stars on a spelling test. Other times,
you wish your kid wouldn't bother you, like when he's whin-
ing over a battle with his big sister. Similarly, our receptivity
to these interruptions varies depending on what is absorbing
us at the moment. There are times when it's easy to change
focus and zero in on our child. Other times, our adult concerns
seem so weighty that unless our kid's hair is on fire, we don't
want to be interrupted.

This copywriter discovered the rewards of understanding his
children's schedule:

I'm a freelance writer, working out of the house. One of the
things I discovered about our 7- to 10-year-old kids is that

*their availability is limited, too. They come home from school
and there's this period when they are totally open to interacting with me. They're no longer at school but not yet transi-
tioned to being at home. They're pulling out bread and
peanut butter and jam, putting school stuff away, and getting
home stuff out. And then fifteen or twenty minutes later,
they're out looking for their friends to play with or in some
other way engaged. So I make it a point to give our kids
attention at their times. I'm ready to get up from my type-
writer when their keys go into the door. My learning is, "I'm
the adult. I'm the one who needs to adapt to when they're
open to interacting."*

When you resent your children's interruptions, it's time to
step back and ask yourself how much time they're really asking
for. Many of their needs can be satisfied in a very few minutes.
How long does it take to take a close look at your daughter's
drawing, ask some questions about the indeterminate shape in
the corner, and comment on the original use of colors? Pulling
your child on your lap for a kiss and a snuggle can be accomplished in the span of a hundred heartbeats. Discussing ways to
handle a bully at school might take less than half an hour, yet
that conversation could become guidance that your child
relies on for the rest of his or her life.

Leave Your Work at Work

*Teach your children to remind you, "But, Daddy, I'm only going
to be young once!"*
Anonymous

Sometimes we aren't open to our children's needs because
even though we're at home our minds are still at the job. It's
hard not to carry work burdens through the front door with us.
So it's important to learn how to let go and reenter our home
lives unencumbered. One doctor I know takes a shower the
moment she comes home. She literally washes away her workday. A friend of mine sits in his car in the driveway and fin-
ishes his to-do list for the next day. Once everything is written
down, he can greet his family with his whole attention.

Commuting via subway or bus can also be a way to shift
gears, as it is for this father:

*I particularly like public transit. I can read on the way to and
from work. It's much less stressful and more productive than
driving in commuter traffic. The bus runs by the top of our
block. And in the evening as I walk down the hill from the bus
stop, I mentally appreciate the quiet neighborhood in which we
live.*

This Balanced Life student tells how she changed her routine and made a tremendous improvement on her family life:

*I used to commute for an hour, then pick up my kids at day
care, then come home and start cleaning, cooking, making
phone calls, etc. Well, not anymore. I pick the kids up and*

come home and sit right down on the floor with them for at least thirty minutes before I do anything else. We laugh and wrestle and play ring-around-the-rosie. This has made a tremendous difference in their attitude, and I find I can do all the chores once they go to bed.

Make the Most of the Time You Have

At the worst, a house unkept cannot be so distressing as a life unlived.
Rose Macaulay

Using timesaving techniques at home is as important as using them in the office. You've worked very hard to get yourself out of the office so you can spend more time at home. The next challenge is to make the most of those hours at home.

One of the most effective ways to create more time for your family is by delegating. Delegating is particularly easy these days, since entire industries and product lines have been created to do the work that stay-at-home women used to do. Plus, by using a little creativity you can also get your children to take on "your" chores, as this woman has:

I don't make the lunches anymore. We now have lunch-making "meetings" at night. Three lunch boxes, three kids making and packing lunches, and Mom asking questions about homework, future assignments, and what's up for the week. I've also given up on having homemade everything—those prepeeled carrots are a miracle. I hired a housecleaner. I have let go.

A good rule of thumb is to delegate away as many of the time-consuming and undesirable chores as you can afford. Hiring a housecleaning service, even one or two times a month, can make a tremendous difference in the quantity and quality of time you have to devote to your family. And if you feel guilty when your family doesn't dine on 100% home-cooked meals, remember that sixty years ago, many people wore home-sewn clothes. If you can get over the guilt of not being the family seamstress, you can recover from not being the family cook.

Prioritizing also ensures that you're dedicating your time to what matters most when you're at home. Sometimes, the most important priority can be just appreciating what you have, like this dad does:

When I find myself still distracted by my workday after I'm home, and feeling the need to "do things while they're on my mind," I like to look at my little girl and remind myself that she won't always be little and desirous of my attention. The day will get here far too soon when she'll be too busy and involved in her own life to spend much time with her father. This seems to do the trick. I'll always have work to do, but my little girl won't stay little forever. I've got to make every moment with her count.

Simplifying and eliminating various tasks will also free up your time for what is truly important. Are you doing all those chores because you want to or, like this mother, because you feel you "should"?

I've found myself trying to let go of my "shoulds." For instance, I should send out holiday cards; I should bake desserts versus buying them for a dinner party; I should see/call certain friends x number of times; etc. In letting go of the "shoulds," I've made more time for my family and myself.

When you find yourself overloaded with chores, ask yourself if they really are important for *you* to do. If they are, then muster your discipline and do them. On the other hand, if they aren't important, then don't commit to them in the first place. The ability to say "No" to yourself and others is just as crucial to your family life as it is in your work life.

Life's Never Perfect

Be kind, for everyone you meet is fighting a hard battle.

Plato

As you try to manage the multiple demands of your job and parenting, remember that nothing will ever be flawless. By deciding to work and to have children, you've chosen a complex yet wondrous path for yourself. But there may be times when it seems like your world is spinning out of control. You scream at your son when he knocks a jar of taco sauce onto the kitchen floor. You get behind at work and miss an important deadline. Your spouse forgets to pick up the dry cleaning, again. When these daily debacles happen, take a deep breath and try to get some perspective on the situation. Are you at risk of losing your job? Even worse, are you at risk of losing someone you love? If you can answer "No" to each of those questions, then your troubles are not so terrible. Next ask yourself if what you're worried about will matter in six months. If not, then you're over another hurdle. Your problems should seem smaller already, and in all likelihood, you are able to solve them.

However, before you race off to take care of whatever is vexing you, take a moment to be kind to yourself. You stand at the epicenter between your work and your family. It is a spot that is filled with so many pressures, stresses, and strains that it would try the spirit of any human being. Remind yourself that every day you do what you can with what you have, and no one should expect more from you than that.

Also, take a moment to savor the fact that you live in a home where people love you and you love them. When you go home, leave your job behind. Be present for the people who live there. If sometime during your day, you've acted in a way that is less than ideal, then forgive yourself. If someone has mistreated you, then forgive him. Let go of what happened in the past and enjoy the evening the universe has granted you. Give your children a hug and yourself one too, and let the enchantment of your family restore your soul.

Exploration Exercises

Looking in the Mirror
Between the challenge of doing well on a job and the mechanics of caring for dependent young ones, we working parents sometimes get distracted from the relationship we have with our child. Familiar patterns become habits, and whether good or bad, they perpetuate themselves without being evaluated. To get a sense of your behavior patterns with your family, do the following exercise.

Think of a typical evening at home. Imagine someone is

holding a video camera and starts filming you the moment you walk in the door. What would be captured on that videotape?

- What time are you coming home?
- What is your demeanor?
- How do you greet your child(ren) when you come in?
- Would the tape capture any conversation between you? What is that conversation like?
- Would the video show you eating together?
- Before your child(ren) goes to sleep, do you say good night? If so, how?

Now, rerun that video in your mind. How do you feel as you watch it? Are there any changes you'd like to make?

Commute Questions

(These questions are for you to ponder when you are commuting, waiting in line, etc. Think of them as directed daydreams.)

- How can you use your end-of-day commute time to close the door on your workday so you can be 100% present for your family once you get home?
- Think about your five Personal Priorities. Are you neglecting those that aren't directly tied to your work or family? Is there a way you can focus more on those, perhaps by incorporating them into your family life in some way? Or are you at a stage in your life when family and work are so time consuming that your other Priorities will have to wait patiently in the background?

Action Step

What weekly tradition would work for your family? Make a list of five. Experiment with one for two or three weeks and see if it improves your family's time together.

> To me, having a balanced life means being able to tell my child, my parents, my postman, my spouse, my grocer, God, my landlady, or a stranger on a bus what I do for a living and as a parent—without any regret or shame.
>
> A part-time writer and mother of one

No Kids, No Spouse, No Balance—How Come?

CINDERELLA MISSES THE PARTY

Cinderella's stepsisters have already left for the prince's ball, and she remains behind mopping the kitchen floor. Suddenly her fairy godmother appears and tells her to get ready for she's going to the ball as well. To the fairy's surprise, Cinderella is not enthusiastic.

"I really want to finish this floor," says Cinderella. "I hate leaving work unfinished. Besides, when my stepmother returns and sees what a good job I've done, she might increase my responsibilities." The godmother points out that the floor isn't so important and this is Cinderella's chance to go out and meet people, maybe even the prince. Besides, Cinderella's stepsisters are at the ball and she has every right to be there, too.

"The truth is," Cinderella counters, "I like it here in the kitchen. The dog and the cat are wonderful friends and it's so warm and peaceful here. I don't want to go to the ball." With that, the fairy godmother flies off, leaving Cinderella alone with her mop.

How often do you find it easier to spend your hours at work than to develop other dimensions of your life?

In many ways it's harder to have balance in your life if you don't have a family at home than if you do. At first this seems paradoxical. Unless they're caring for aging parents, why would unmarried, childless people have problems with balance? After all, they can devote all the time they need to their jobs without feeling conflicted by family responsibilities.

At one time I was convinced that the people who struggled most for balance in today's society were working mothers with children, in other words, women like me. In fact, when I was preparing to teach my first Balanced Life workshop, I designed my lesson plan to meet the needs of those moms. When I walked into that first class, however, I saw that half the attendees were men, and it dawned on me that I'd made an inaccurate assumption. I then asked how many people had children living at home. Out of a group of twenty-five people, three hands went up. So much for my enlightening lesson on how to find balance when you work and have kids! I ad-libbed through most of that class and then rewrote the plans for the rest of my lectures.

Since then, every class and lecture I've held has attracted people who have neither a spouse nor children and who still don't devote enough time to their home lives. I've learned that family-related responsibilities can be very effective in prying people away from their jobs at a reasonable hour. Without that counterbalancing force, work can take over your life completely.

While I wrote this chapter specifically for single people with no children, you may find that parts of it ring true even if you don't fit that category. Married people whose spouses are absent for long periods of time or parents whose children aren't living at home may also face conditions similar to those

I'm describing. For the ease of communication, however, I'll address this chapter to the single and childless among you and presume that everyone else will apply any lessons that are appropriate.

Avoiding Those After-Hours Assignments

Time is the coin of your life. It is the only coin you have, and only you can determine how it will be spent. Be careful lest you let other people spend it for you.

Carl Sandburg

In many organizations, bosses and co-workers presume that since you don't have a spouse or children, nothing critical is going on in your life. Therefore, you can be expected to work longer and less desirable hours than anyone else. This logic proclaims that the privilege of leaving work is directly corre-lated to the degree of complexity in your family life. Carried to an extreme, this reasoning becomes absurd. The single parent with three kids works 6-hour days, the two-career couple with a new baby works 7-hour days, the person with a stay-at-home spouse and two children works 9-hours days, and the single, childless person (God bless him or her!) can work 12-hour days.

An unmarried service representative writes,

I do think there is an unspoken expectation that single people should pick up the slack sometimes. I've experienced a num-ber of occasions when I was expected to work the holidays or be on call just because I was single and without children.

The attitude that unmarried people should labor longer is sometimes expressed in irrational ways, as told by this newlywed:

> I was the most junior person in my office, so unofficially it was my job to finish off all the loose ends at the end of the day. But then I got married, and as soon as I got back from my honeymoon, the attitude of my co-workers totally changed. Suddenly they were encouraging me to go home in the evening so I could spend time with my husband. The irony is that my husband and I had been living together long before we got married. Due to some unknown logic, the ring on my finger gave me the right to go home.

The truth is, no company has the right to adjust your workload based on the conditions of your personal life. Single or married, with or without children, you have an obligation to accomplish a certain amount of work for your job. If your family life is burdened with multiple obligations, you need to learn ways to do your job and fulfill your responsibilities at home. It's not fair to expect others in your workplace to do part of your job for you. Of course, we all know that emergencies happen and sometimes co-workers have to pitch in. But those emergencies can happen to anyone, whether or not you have children at home.

So what should you do if you're a single person and your office mates or supervisors assume you are available for all of the after-hour or weekend assignments? Different situations require different responses, but one of the most effective is for you to say, "I have a commitment." In nine cases out of ten, those four simple words end all further discussion, as this woman learned:

I found that once I say I have a commitment, my co-workers are more respectful of my time. They almost never question what the commitment is for—I think they assume it is an Ob-Gyn appointment and so they're afraid to ask.

Sometimes you'll encounter a boss or co-worker who wants to know what your commitment is so he or she can evaluate its importance versus the work that needs to be done. Resist this probing if you can. After all, you're the one who best knows what work needs to be done compared to the importance of your commitment to yourself. Remember, the less you say and the fewer excuses you make, the more apt you are to get your own way.

Other times you may find that making allies of your boss or colleagues can be an effective strategy. This may be particularly useful if you work in a small office where everybody's aware of each other's comings and goings. Sharing your passion, whether it's for triathlon running, Japanese ceramics, or volunteer work at a hospice, helps others understand that you are as committed to your Personal Priorities as they are to their families.

Three Reasons Why Single People Work Too Much

We have but one life—whether we spend it laughing or weeping.
Anonymous

It is not only supervisors and co-workers who perpetuate the myth that you must be totally work focused if you haven't a family. Single people with no children are often co-conspirators in their own lack of balance. There are three main reasons that as an unmarried person with no children, you might have a tendency to devote especially long hours to your job: career advancement, the satisfaction you feel when you are at your workplace, and/or the tendency to minimize your own needs for balance.

Reason 1: You Want to Advance Your Career

By working faithfully eight hours a day, you may eventually get to be
a boss and work twelve hours a day.
Robert Frost

Demographically, you are more apt to be unmarried and child-less in the early stages of your career. Ambition and enthusiasm for a job can dominate your life. When you're young, you believe there is always time for everything. Developing relationships, a family, and outside interests can wait while you scramble up those first steps of the career ladder. Balance is just not a priority.

In fact, this might be the ideal period in your life to concentrate on your job and "pay your dues." When I was in my 20s, single, and living in New York City, I often worked until 9 P.M. and then went home to my apartment for a solitary meal of scrambled eggs or Chinese noodles. I didn't have a boyfriend, or hardly even a date, which was probably the result of overwork. (Of course, I rarely had a boyfriend or a date before I was a workaholic in New York, but I'd rather blame my lack of a social life on overdedication to my job than to a distressing dearth of popularity.)

At some point, most people want more in their lives than just their work. This is especially important if you aren't committed to living a single lifestyle for the foreseeable future. Ask yourself: if you stay on the path you're on, are you truly creating the life you want?

When this MBA examined his work situation, he knew he had to make changes:

After I graduated I found a great, but very demanding job. My initial reaction was I'm young and have the stamina to survive on only four or five hours of sleep a night. However, after two years of eating the majority of my dinners at work and taking cabs home because the el had stopped running, I decided that experiencing the better portion of my 20s from the inside of an office was not what I wanted to do. I decided to find a job that would allow me free time in the evenings to do what I wanted—date, work out, take classes, and generally just enjoy being outdoors.

Reason 2: Your Workplace Provides All You Want

The universe is full of magical things patiently waiting
for our wits to grow sharper.
Eden Phillpots

Sometimes single, childless people work extra-long hours because they genuinely enjoy their work environment. Let's face it, work can be seductive, particularly when there's no special someone to attract you away. A good job with a great company brings intellectual challenge, comradeship, a sense of accomplishment, and stimulation to your life. There are goals to strive for, competitors to beat, people to talk to, and people to talk about. The office becomes your "home" and your co-workers become your "family." If the alternative is to go to an empty apartment and the television set, why wouldn't you stay at work?

This fashion buyer expresses the feelings that many people have about their jobs:

> I live for my job—I absolutely love it. I am my work. It's my passion and I don't want to do anything else. I love the people, the travel, the excitement. I can't imagine that I am so lucky to find work that let me be so completely myself.

Unfortunately, like most seductions, those provided by work lose their attractiveness as time goes on. For most of us, the delight in devoting weekends to complete a project becomes stale after a while. Or you feel martyred and underappreciated for your many heroic efforts. And sometimes denying yourself time for rest or renewal results in chronic illnesses or depression.

Besides, you will eventually discover that work rarely passes muster as a long-term substitute for a personal life. As management philosophies change, as companies grow or contract or are taken over, and as the people you enjoy working with move on, workplaces can evolve from delightful environments to those that aren't fun anymore. If you build your personal life exclusively within this changing world, you are setting yourself up for an inevitable disappointment.

Reason 3: You Downplay Your Need for Balance

All the animals except man know that the principal business
of life is to enjoy it.
Samuel Butler

You may be one of those people who buy into the notion that it's more important for others to be with their families than it is for you to have a home life. As a single person without children, you view much of what you do outside of work as optional. Canceling your dinner date creates fewer repercussions for you than your co-worker would face if her son were home unsupervised. You might admire your colleague's desire to go home to his or her spouse (and may even feel a little envious), and so you volunteer to be the one who stays late. In short, as you weigh your needs against those of others, yours always come up a bit light.

One accountant described her situation to me this way:

I often find myself working alone in the office because everybody else has gone home to their families. Sometimes I wonder if I should go home too, but then I ask, why? After all, if I do go home, no one cares but the cat.

Occasionally, single people minimize their need for balance because they view their lifestyle as a temporary phenomenon. They claim that they'll start living the lives they dream of when they become involved in a serious relationship, but not necessarily before. In the meanwhile, they choose to slight their other Priorities in order to dedicate their waking hours to work. If this applies to you, it may be time to take a more critical look at your situation, like this attorney did:

> *I suddenly realized there was nothing in my life but sleep and my job. I would get up, go to work, and eventually come home. I told myself I didn't have the time to go to the gym, I didn't have time for friends, I didn't have time for anything but my job. Then I asked myself: what would my life be like if I never got out of this rut? One of these days I want to have a husband and children. I wasn't going to find them while I was working 60-hour weeks.*

Working a 60-hour week is not just a tremendous commitment of time; it is also a commitment of emotional energy. Most people find maintaining that pace leaves them drained and devoid of enthusiasm for anything else. When you put in so many hours that the weekend finds you with as much spark as a dead battery, how do you expect to cultivate the aspects of your personality that aren't associated with work? Maybe it's time to change your habits and recommit yourself to the life you have outside of the workplace.

There are times when these rationalizations for working longer hours—wanting to advance your career, finding contentment at your workplace, or minimizing your own needs for balance—make perfect sense. The problems arise, however, when this pattern turns into a lifelong habit. When that happens, your social life, health, and learning opportunities all become secondary to work and balance is another New Year's resolution that you'll never achieve.

Getting Into the Habit of Balance

The doors we open and close each day decide the lives we live.
Flora Whittlemore

Once you decide to break away from the workaholic lifestyle, you may find that you need to develop some techniques that'll keep you from backsliding into familiar patterns. One man, who had "Having good friends, being a good friend" as a Personal Priority, told me of his self-monitoring device:

My home answering machine flashes a red light when a message is waiting for me. When I come home and the light isn't blinking, my first reaction is to think that nobody cares about me. But then I realize that I've probably been too involved in work and haven't reached out to the people I know. So I'll start making a few calls and sure enough, my answering machine will light up again.

A businesswoman found another way to ensure more balance to her life:

It took a long time for the truth to come to me, but I finally realized that I was never home because there was nothing for me there. Every night I'd work late, hang out with friends, or attend gallery openings, not because I was dying to go but because I didn't want to face my empty apartment. Once I could put my finger on the problem, the solution was easy. It may sound silly, yet it's true . . . I got a puppy. Now it's fun to be home.

Maybe you've already tried to develop interests outside of work, but none of them seem to stick. Your health club membership has expired, you stopped attending watercolor classes, and you dropped out of the softball league. It seems that no matter what you've attempted, work is always more interesting, more urgent, and somehow just more important. If this is happening to you, now is a good time to review your Personal Priorities. Which of them are workplace oriented and which of them have to be developed away from the job? If none of them requires nurturing outside of work, maybe what you're doing is right for you. On the other hand, if even one of your Personal Priorities is best pursued when you're not at work, nudge yourself away from your job and do something about it. Your earlier attempts to find outside interests may have bombed because you tried activities that weren't particularly important to you.

This manager found that volunteer work provided him with the impetus to leave the office at a reasonable hour:

There have been times in the past where I felt it was expected that I put in more hours than a married person with children, since I didn't have other "obligations." So I got involved in activities outside of work. I spent several years chairing a committee for a nonprofit organization, which allowed me to leave on time, or early in some cases, to support the organization.

Deciding What You Want From Life

You create your opportunities by asking for them.
Patty Hansen

If you still find yourself conflicted about wanting to work less and yet not being able to identify an activity you'd rather do, consider creating a Five-Year Forecast for yourself. I describe this exercise more thoroughly at the end of the chapter, but fundamentally it entails nothing more than writing down what you want to bring about in your life over the next five years. Don't limit your list to accomplishments or achievements. Include your hopes for relationships and experiences. Your list might contain major goals, like becoming a best-selling novelist, or just romantic notions, like spending a week in a mountain cabin.

Sitting down and writing your list serves two purposes. First, it fires up your imagination and will inspire you to achieve at least one of your wishes in the near future. Second, putting your dreams down on paper creates a subconscious commitment that'll make achieving all of them more apt to happen.

Deciding what you want from life can be very powerful and set off changes that you never thought would happen to you. A paralegal writes,

Travel and buying a home were both things that were high on my list. I didn't really believe I could afford either, but I decided to try. I leave for Italy on April 29 and will be gone until June. (My boss initially freaked, even though I had the

vacation time coming. Now she's telling me how much I deserve it. . . . I think she envies me.) I also have done some looking around for houses, and realize that there are options out there for me, so that's in the plans by the end of the year.

It is surprising how paying attention to your wishes can change your life for the better, as this budding author found:

Doing these exercises has helped to inspire me to have a balanced life and to write a book. I have made a point of leaving work at 5 or 5:30 P.M.—something I have never done in my entire adult life. Now I have sufficient energy to take on "projects of the heart" that inspire me, rather than just resting up for another grueling week of work. I'm in the early stages of doing research on my passion: San Francisco architecture. I plan to write a book of walking tours, focusing especially on neighborhoods with Victorian homes.

Being single and childless creates a set of opportunities and occasional drawbacks that differ from those experienced by people who are married and/or have children. What's not different, however, is the need to expand your life outside the workplace. No matter how interesting, challenging, or satisfying a job might be, in the long term it won't be enough to help you develop your fullest potential or joy as a human being. Getting into the habit of creating and valuing balance will enrich your life, no matter who does or doesn't wait for you at home.

Exploration Exercises

Looking in the Mirror

As I mentioned earlier in this chapter, creating a Five-Year Forecast is an excellent way to nudge your life along in the direction you want it to go.

This is an audio-visualization exercise because instead of asking you to visualize a particular scene, I'm going to ask you to imagine a conversation with a friend. As in the last "visualization" exercise, this technique is most effective if you can hear the instructions while you are relaxed with your eyes closed. If you can't find someone to read it to you, read it into a cassette recorder and play it back for yourself. Or read it to yourself and then try to "hear" the conversation. You can also listen to a variation of this meditation on my Web site: www.comingupforair.com.

After you have heard this conversation in your mind, take out a pen and paper. Write down your answers to the questions your friend asked. You've just created a list of what you want to happen in your life over the next five years.

Commute Questions

(These questions are for you to ponder when you are commuting, waiting in line, etc. Think of them as directed daydreams.)

As you review your Five-Year Forecast, is there any particular area that you aren't confident you can achieve? Perhaps it's one that you have already been wrestling with without success. Choose the item that creates the most doubts for you, and play out the following conversation in your mind. If need be, keep thinking about this over several days.

CREATING YOUR FIVE-YEAR FORECAST

Sit comfortably in a chair. Take a deep breath. Now close your eyes and take another deep breath. Listen to the noises around you as you continue to breathe deeply.

Imagine that five years have passed by. Think about what year it is. How old are you now? If you are in the same job, how many years have you been there altogether? If you are living in the same place, how many years have you been there?

Now imagine that the phone rings and it is a friend you have lost touch with over the last five years. Think about who that might be and hear his or her voice.

You are delighted to talk to your friend again and eager to catch up, for in fact, the last five years have been a wonderful time for you. Your friend asks you the following questions. Listen to your voice answering the questions.

- *Your friend asks:* What's been happening in your personal life? What good stuff has been going on?
  You respond:
- *Your friend asks:* Are you still working like you were five years ago? What got you to change?
  You respond:
- *Your friend asks:* What's been going on with the other parts of your life (i.e., travel, volunteer work, hobbies, going back to school)?
  You respond:
- *Your friend asks:* What else good has happened in the last five years?
  You respond:

After you have finished answering your friend's questions, take two more deep breaths. Now open your eyes.

Again, it's five years in the future. The same friend is pleased and surprised that you finally achieved that particular objective. He or she says, "I'm so happy to hear that! Congratulations! Tell me how it happened."

You answer your friend, giving step-by-step details about how you managed to achieve what had seemed to be a difficult goal.

(Don't ask me to explain the academic theory behind this exercise, but it works. You start in the future, when you have achieved your goal, and then work backward. For some reason, once you presume you've hit your objective, it's easier to understand how you did it.)

Action Step

Take a look at everything you listed for your Five-Year Forecast. Now pick one item and think how you can use next week's gift of time to bring that item closer to reality.

If you are feeling particularly motivated, you can also fill out the following chart.

WHERE I AM NOW	WHERE I WANT TO BE (TAKE THIS FROM YOUR FIVE-YEAR FORECAST)	WHAT I CAN DO IN AN HOUR IN THE NEXT WEEK(S) TO MAKE MY FORECAST MORE LIKELY TO COME TRUE

> To me, having a balanced life means that at the end of the week, I've touched upon all the elements of my life that are important: had daily conversations with God, made meaningful contributions at work, been in touch with my parents, spent at least one evening talking on the phone or having dinner with a friend, made a few journal entries, and had a few workouts at the gym.
>
> A formerly married businesswoman

How to Change Jobs and Keep a Balanced Life

SEEKING THE QUIETER SKY

A seagull grabs a crust of bread left on the beach by picnickers. As he flies away, other gulls flock around him, trying to steal the bread. They chase him relentlessly, until finally he decides to let go of the crust. As it falls, the other birds plunge after it.

"Well," says the first gull philosophically, "I may have lost the crust of bread, but I have regained a peaceful sky."

Is the prize you cling to so tightly worth the price of your happiness?

What happens if your current work environment is clashing so much with your balanced life that you decide to quit? Or what if you have created a balanced life in one work situation but want to move on to another job? How do you have the lifestyle you desire and still have a satisfying career?

Your challenge is to find a job that meets your career needs and allows you the freedom to develop your other priorities as well. This might mean work hours that begin and end at reasonable times. For some people, it suggests working for an organization whose values are consistent with theirs, as was the case with this banker:

> *I was doing very well at the bank where I was working. I was one of the youngest VPs and had lots of opportunities to get on the fast track. But I hated it! I saw sanctioned manipulation of employees and customers where people actually lied in the service of their own political and personal gains. I spent a year agonizing about it while still working there. When I finally walked out, I was so confused I didn't want to sign up with another corporation. Instead I went backpacking for seven months. Once I came home again, a friend recommended the company I work for now. Happily its values are much more in tune with mine.*

Making the Break from Your Old Job

A pitcher cries for water to carry and a person for work that is real.
Marge Piercy

No matter what reason compels you to make the move, you'll find that venturing into the job market is hard work. In the first place, you're opening yourself to being evaluated by strangers. The chance of rejection is high and rejection always hurts. Second, when you look elsewhere you take on a certain risk in your current position. As you start imagining better situations, your present job becomes even less bearable. There's also the chance that your employer may find out and be less than tickled to know you're thinking of leaving. The third concern is that starting a job hunt takes a lot of time, something you don't have. To conduct a good job search, you have to evaluate your skills, experiences, and needs, find companies you want to work for, and then identify the people within that company who might be able to hire you. Lastly, there is the interview process itself. All in all, hours and hours are poured into the job-hunting process and taken from your other Priorities.

Despite the burden you take on while looking for a new job, the price you pay for not looking can be even worse. This office worker tells the story of pushing herself to the thin edge of what she could handle before she realized she needed a different approach:

When I first started at my current company, I really wanted to do as well as I possibly could. I worked late five days a week. Now I have a 13-year-old daughter at home and am a single parent. Plus, I'm going through an incredibly challenging personal period in my life as a result of the divorce process. When my daughter's grades started to slip, my own stamina diminished, and I was simply exhausted at the end of each week. I finally realized that I was working too long, too hard. I had to shift my priorities, or else!

It took some time, but I decided that the position I was initially hired for was not a good fit for me anymore. Then I researched my options, and transferred into another job. I also set a daily goal of taking lunch for at least a half hour just to get out and walk. Finally, I made a choice of going home on time unless it was absolutely necessary to stay late. As a result, my daughter's grades improved because of the time I was able to spend with her on her homework. I also found that my energy level went up because I now made time to exercise. My productivity at work increased dramatically because I was in a position that helped me balance my work/family life.

This woman was able to change jobs within the same firm and create more balance in her life. This type of job transfer is generally easier than switching to a brand-new firm. If your dissatisfaction centers on a dictatorial boss or a particularly frenzied job, maybe there's another niche within the company you're already working for. Look for opportunities there first— you might discover a great situation with minimal effort. If that isn't feasible, however, then you'll have to launch yourself into the outside world.

Discovering the Right Job

Your work is to discover your work and then with all your heart
give yourself to it.
Buddha

To find a work environment that fits your needs requires a good sense of what those needs are. Then you have to learn all you can about prospective employers. Each step is important and neither particularly hard to do if you get some guidance and take the time to ask the right questions. (My favorite publications on changing jobs are listed in the "Suggested Reading" section at the end of this book.)

Judging your own needs is simply a continuation of the work you've done so far in creating more balance in your life. As you think about entering a new job, how does it relate to your Personal Priorities? You need to be sure that your next job allows you time to pursue them.

The next step is to review what motivates you. Once you understand what rewards—emotional or monetary—drive you, you can be alert to whether or not your new workplace uses techniques that will complement your makeup. If you do your best in a competitive environment, pursue that in an employer. On the other hand, if you outdo yourself when striving for a fat bonus, look for that in your new organization.

As a final step in the self-evaluation process, think about your ambition and where it's pulling you as you embark on a job search. Are you feeling torn, with one part of you wanting more time to spend on your home life and another part wanting a job that is more stimulating, prestigious, and financially rewarding than what you have right now? There's nothing wrong in wanting a more challenging job, but it may require more time than your current job. Is that a trade-off you want to make? Conversely, you may find that your ambition is losing momentum, that your other Personal Priorities have become so compelling you're willing to make fewer trade-offs for a job. Maybe this is the time to reevaluate your geographic choices and find a job that keeps you close to your true home. Or perhaps you're ready to find a job that frees you to spend the time you want on your artistic ventures, like this woman was able to do:

> Working part time is the answer to my search for balance. I have a deep desire to pursue my dance and choreography. I also want to dedicate myself more fully to travel, my spiritual practices, and my community service. Being a part-timer works very well for me. The flexibility it affords in my life is priceless.

Being honest with yourself about what you want from a job change is crucial to landing on a spot that you'll like. If you disregard the aspects of life and work that are truly important to you, gloss over the motivators that help you excel, or

obscure the trade-offs you are willing to make for your ambition, only luck will lead you to a new job that will make you
happy.

Scoping Out a New Work Environment

God gives food to every bird, but does not throw it into the nest.
Montenegrin proverb

Of course, understanding yourself is not enough to find the
position that provides the balance you need. You also need to
analyze your potential workplace. It is only under rare circumstances that you will find any written materials which give a
true picture of how a particular company supports its employees' need for balance. Annual reports, employee manuals,
recruiting brochures, and other corporate propaganda may
promote the company's respect for employees, but be skepti-
cal. No firm is going to confess that their philosophy is to
squeeze every ounce of substance out of their workers, only to
discard the exhausted husk.

For more objective sources, check out the magazines that
regularly publish surveys listing companies that support work
and family. These include *Working Mothers'* "100 Best Companies for Working Mothers," *Fortune Magazine's* "100 Best
Companies to Work for in America," and *Business Week's*
"Best Companies for Work and Family." However, these surveys cover a relatively small number of firms and only the ones
large enough to have human resource departments that will
bother to fill out the questionnaire.

Be aware that philosophies about employee relations can
vary widely within larger companies. Someone may describe a

work environment that you would love, but unless you work within that same area or even for the same boss, your experience might be disappointing.

Look, Listen, and Learn

You can see a lot by observing.
Yogi Berra

Since outside resources are inadequate, you need to bank on the direct approach. Luckily, interviewing provides you with the perfect opportunity to observe the work space and ask questions. As you go to interviews, think of yourself as Sherlock Holmes or Mata Hari and see what clues you can pick up about the culture. Are people racing down the corridors faster than the White Rabbit in *Alice in Wonderland*? Do you hear any laughter, especially the kind that comes from the heart and not nervous outbursts? What awards or motivational posters are on the walls? Is there a Polaroid of the winner of the "Workaholic of the Week" contest? You can tell a lot about a work environment by keeping your eyes open. Don't be afraid to gawk. This job seeker picked up a warning from something as innocuous as family photos:

At one of the firms I was interviewing with, I noticed there weren't many photographs of families in any of the managers' offices. The few photos I saw were formal portraits with the husband, wife, and children neatly arranged on a couch or stairway. At the other company I was considering, most of the offices had lots of photos of families and kids. One man had a picture of himself and a Little League team. I asked if he coached, and when he said yes, I was able to ask him about how he was able to leave in the afternoon for practice and still get his work done. Our conversation reassured me that this was a firm that's used to giving employees flexibility in their hours.

In addition to exercising your eyeballs, be sure to ask a lot of questions of the people you interview with. The point of these questions is to get them to describe the true culture of the place while not having them perceive you as a slacker. Some of my favorite questions are these:

SAMPLE QUESTIONS TO EVALUATE A NEW JOB ENVIRONMENT

1. *Think of a person who has a position either similar to or the same as the one I am interviewing for. Can you describe a typical day?*
   In addition to giving you a good sense of what the new job might be like, this question may also give you some ideas about expected start and quitting times.
2. *Would you mind telling me what is a typical day for you? (Good to ask of your potential boss or colleagues. It's useless to ask it of the HR person.)*
   Again, listen for start and end times. If the boss comes in at dawn and leaves after 8 at night, she might not be open to employees who value balance.
3. *How long have you been looking to fill this position? Are there other open positions in the department?*
   Try to find out if the staffing shortages are due to growth or excessive turnover. The answers might reveal that this area suffers from chronic under-staffing (a bad environment for someone who's looking for balance) or a work environment that drives staff members away (an even worse environment if you're looking for balance).

4. *I currently have a number of commitments on weekends and some evenings. If I take this job, would I need to adjust those commitments?*

Listen carefully to the tone of this answer as well as the words. If the company is interested in you, they may not want to scare you off by telling you the truth about the number of hours they expect.

This question is also very useful because it introduces the fact that you do have priorities in your life other than work. Later, if you find you are being pressured to work unreasonable hours on a regular basis, you can refer back to this conversation as one of the factors that shaped your decision to take the job.

5. *Sometimes I find that I'm more productive if I work at home one or two days a month. It helps me get away from the interruptions of the office and concentrate on what needs to be done. Does that approach make sense for this job? Can you give me an example of someone who does that now?* (This question may not apply in all circumstances.)

It doesn't matter if you have or haven't worked at home or even if you would enjoy such an option. You want to learn if this is a workplace that evaluates employees by the work they produce instead of by the number of hours they are visible in the office. Don't be afraid to probe a bit. If your interviewer says it's OK for you to work at home, ask for an example of someone who does it. If he can't name names, be suspicious.

6. *How is this organization involved in the local community? For example, are there employee volunteer groups that assist the public schools?*

With this question, you're scrutinizing the values of the organization. Do they see themselves as having any responsibilities beyond their own marketplace? Generally (although not always) companies that encourage their employees' volunteer efforts are also understanding about a person's other priorities.

As you're deciding whether the work environment and job are attractive to you, you also need to demonstrate that you're the type of person they're dying to hire. Since you can't sell yourself as a 60-hour-a-week workaholic, you need to stress how you're a person who works smart rather than long. Once again, you can polish up the timesaving techniques and explain how you have used prioritizing, delegating, simplifying, and so on, to achieve the objectives of your job. The more you can cite specific examples with clear payoffs for the company, the more attractive you will be as a potential employee.

'Fessing Up to Your Need for Balance

This above all: to thine own self be true.
William Shakespeare

As you and a prospective employer edge closer and closer to finding each other, there comes a point when you should talk about your need to spend time on your nonwork-related priorities. The degree and the timing of your disclosure depend a lot on how constraining your other priorities are. If you just want to be on your way home at a reasonable hour most evenings, a general discussion about typical workdays will suffice. On the other hand, if you are a single father and your child-care situation leaves you no flexibility for extended hours at the workplace, your employer needs to know that before you accept a job. From your point of view, you may prefer to mention any time constraints after the company actually puts an offer on the table. However, you don't want to start a relationship with new employers by handing them a rude surprise just as they think they're closing the deal. If you've been doing your interviewing correctly, you should already have a sense of the firm's reaction to your desire for balance. But don't accept the job assuming everything will work out—if you have specific time restrictions, tell them. If they react poorly, it is not the right job for you anyway.

This story told to me by a software engineer is one of my favorite examples of how you can be up front about your need for balance and still land the job you want:

> I was interviewing for a great job with a great career opportunity. My concern was that it might demand more time than I was willing to provide. At the end of that first interview, I told the hiring manager not to schedule any additional interviews if my "face time" at the office was a potential problem. This was a risk because I wanted the position, but my personal goals were equally important. Happily, he did arrange additional interviews for me as well as other meetings with him to talk about the actual job responsibilities and required tools (e.g., remote access from my home computer) if I accepted the position. After I accepted, he set expectations around the office about my situation. He didn't include the reason why, which was because I had to be home for my son. Instead, he just asked people to be considerate when scheduling early or late meetings. It has worked out great.

Not every job interview will have a happy ending like the one this engineer experienced. It's tough enough to find a job that'll provide you with the right intellectual, emotional, and financial rewards. And you're making the search even harder by demanding that you have time for your home life. Some people will think you're nuts and try to talk you out of it.

Don't listen to them. Tell yourself that perseverance is mandatory. But when you get discouraged, and you will at some point in the process, pull out your Personal Priorities and remind yourself of the person you want to be.

Let Your New Job Be the Right Job

All that matters is love and work.
Sigmund Freud

As I mentioned earlier, looking for a new job can be a long and arduous process. There may come a time in your search when you want to give up and either keep the dreary job you have or take one that is barely passable. I want to encourage you *not* to do that. Throughout this book, I have been talking about how infinitely precious your time is. Together we have tried to find ways to squeeze a measly two or three hours out of your workweek so that you have time for activities that nourish your soul. But think of how many hours are spent on your job. Those hours are valuable, too. At least some of them should bring as much joy to your life as an hour spent on any of your other Priorities.

I consider myself extremely blessed to have had jobs that I've loved at a company I adore. It took me a long time to get there. Until I was 30, I had never lasted at any job longer than eighteen months. With less than ten years' work experience, my résumé listed half a dozen employers and concealed as many stretches of unemployment. But in 1982, I got lucky and stumbled into a company that fit my personality and my work style. With the exception of a year off to write this book, I have been there, loving it, ever since. Well, to be honest, I love it most of the time. Occasionally, I've felt frustrated, overstressed, and underappreciated. Thankfully, those times don't last long and I am soon recharged by the next assignment that comes my way. Having a job I love is key to having a life I love, and having a life you love is what balance is all about.

So as you go about looking for work and balance, take the time you need to understand yourself and the job you really want. Then try with all your might to find what you deserve. Listen to your inner voice and have faith. The search is worth it, for the reward is as large as your life.

Exploration Exercises

Looking in the Mirror

When you are looking for a new job that meets your professional and/or salary needs and you still want a balanced life, it is critical that you believe and can articulate why seeking balance makes you a more productive employee. Preparing your thoughts on this topic in advance makes you ready for any questions. Even if you are not thinking of changing jobs, this exercise is useful because it helps deflects any naysayers who claim you can't have balance and be productive at work.

To get you started, think about the various timesaving techniques we've discussed. Write down specific examples of how you've applied any or all of these techniques to be more efficient and effective at your job:

- Prioritizing
- Delegating
- Simplifying
- Setting time limits

- Procrastinating (given its poor moral connotations, you may want to skip this one in your interview!)
- Eliminating

Commute Questions
(*These questions are for you to ponder when you are commuting, waiting in line, etc. Think of them as directed daydreams.*)

Pull out the Ambition Worksheet you completed for Chapter 4. Review column 2, the area of your life you would not trade off, and column 3, how (if at all) would you like to adjust the trade-offs you have already made. As you go back and forth to work and to job interviews, keep reviewing these points in your mind. Now that you are actually looking for a new job, is there anything you would want to change on that worksheet?

Action Step
Ask a friend or trusted colleague to help you with practice interviewing. Have them ask questions about your commitment to your job and how you demonstrate it. Then you practice asking them the questions you'll use to discover if your new work environment welcomes employees who value balance.

> For me, having a balanced life means having an emotional life as well as a professional life. I know that I've lost my balance when I may still be able to think but I feel so flat and so tired that I stop "experiencing" my family or friends.
>
> A corporate finance and planning officer,
> MBA, and former investment banker

Part 4:

LOOKING FORWARD

Gather ye rosebuds while ye may,

Old Time is still a-flying;

And this same flower that smiles today,

Tomorrow will be dying.

Robert Herrick

Balance as a Lifelong Habit

THE BUSINESSWOMAN AND THE FISHERMAN

A rich businesswoman comes across a fisherman mending his net on the dock during the middle of the day. "Why aren't you out fishing?" she asks.

"I caught all the fish I need for the day," replies the man.

"But if you caught more fish, you could sell them," exhorts the businesswoman. "Then you could buy a better net."

"And what would I do with that?"

"Catch even more fish. Then you buy a bigger boat and go out longer and bring in a really big catch."

"What happens then?" asks the fisherman.

"Why, then you could make lots of money and sit back and really enjoy life," answers the woman.

"What do you think I am doing now?"

*As time goes on, how will you find the balance between
accomplishing your work and enjoying your life?*

This is the last chapter of this book. You have read the techniques and have done some or all of the exercises. Now it is time to put those techniques into practice and enjoy a life that balances your work life and your home life, a life that lets you devote time and energy to your job and to all the other marvelous aspects of life that matter to you.

Changing the way we do things is always a challenge. Particularly when the change is as difficult as building a balanced life in a workaholic world. For a few nights, you leave at your departure hour and relish the pleasures of the evening. It's generally easy to schedule and complete one hour as a gift of time. But as your life gets busy and the work pressures mount, your motivation to create more balance might just slip away.

How do you forestall that slippage? How do you remain true to yourself while your workplace expects you to bend and twist at its command? Now that you've practiced many of the techniques for creating a balanced life, the way to keep them alive is to follow these three guidelines:

1. Remember and honor your Personal Priorities
2. Stay conscious of how you spend your time
3. Keep asking, "Am I making the choices I want?"

Remember and Honor Your Personal Priorities

Things which matter most must never be at the mercy of things which matter least.
Johann von Goethe

Having balance in your life is mostly about priority management; the time management aspects are important but secondary. The most critical question is not how much can you accomplish in an hour. Instead, ask yourself: are you accomplishing what is right for you?

Your Personal Priorities should be your guideposts. You've chosen them as being more important to you than anything else in the world right now. How well do you know what they are? Why not write them down again, here on this page at this moment.

My five Personal Priorities are as follows:

1.

2.

3.

4.

5.

I asked you to write down your Priorities because I want to be sure you know them, that they are ingrained in your consciousness and part of your daily decision-making process. Even as you're reading this chapter, the phone might start ringing or an e-mail may be pending on your computer screen. Someone, somewhere wants your time. They want it for their purposes. And when they ask, you must choose what to say. As long as you choose based on your Personal Priorities, you're building balance in your life. Forget or ignore those Priorities, and a piece of your life is no longer your own.

If you want balance to remain part of your life for the next weeks and months, you need to create an environment in which your Personal Priorities can flourish. The easiest way to do this is to make your calendar your ally. I presume you already have scheduled routines to honor your Priorities, whether time for ukulele lessons, dinner dates with friends, or a commitment to volunteer weekly at the animal shelter. Have you also booked some more extensive events—a weekend at a meditation retreat, a visit with your college roommate, or going camping with your kids? Keep thinking of the person you *want* to be. What events would he or she have on a calendar? Why not make them real for yourself? Schedule your Priorities into your life and enjoy the balance you deserve.

On the last day of every year, office workers in San Francisco rip apart their desk calendars and throw the pages out the window. The air and sidewalk become filled with drifting scraps of paper. Pretend that I was standing under your window on December 31, catching the leaves of your calendar as they fluttered down. Could I tell that you were a person who knows and acts on a set of Personal Priorities? I hope so.

Stay Conscious of How You Spend Your Time

I have spent my days stringing and unstringing my instrument,
while the song I came to sing remains unsung to this day.
Rabindranath Tagore

While the most important factor to having a balanced life is priority management, the second most important is time management. In many ways, time is like money. You can invest it, spend it on something you value, or you can waste it. But unlike money, you can't save it for another day. So as you work to have balance in your life, ask yourself: what have you done with your last few hours? Did you use them as an investment, doing something you didn't particularly enjoy but knowing that a positive payback would result? Were they spent devoted to one of your Personal Priorities, whether at home or at work? Or were they depleted thoughtlessly, dribbled away on some activity that brought neither joy nor peace nor a sense of accomplishment to your life?

Every day each of us is presented with twenty-four hours. Each of us chooses how to spend that time. Demands on that time, like demands on your wallet, always exceed what is available. To create and maintain balance in your life, you have to divide your time wisely, so much for your work life, so much for your home life, so much for rest and renewal. Unfortunately, once you have made those divisions, other people will ask you to change your mind and give your time to them instead.

Remind yourself that people who ask you for your time are like people who beg for money. You don't hand out your money to anyone who asks. Yet when someone requests a piece of your time, are you embarrassed to refuse? Some people presume that your ten minutes can be theirs for the asking. Tell them they are wrong. Those ten minutes belong to you and your Priorities.

Forgive the Past, Trust the Future, Be Present

Worry does not empty tomorrow of its sorrow;
it empties today of its joy.
Anonymous

In addition to the external forces that seek to claim your time, there are also insidious internal forces. These are the twin beasts of regret and worry. Whenever we let these creatures settle in our consciousness, we destroy our capability to enjoy the present. To the degree that you can forgive the past and trust the future, you'll create more time to delight in the life that surrounds you now.

Forgiveness rarely comes easily. It's hard for us to forgive others when they wrong us. Sometimes you might even find it hard to forgive yourself. But without forgiveness, ugly parts of your past sneak back into your day. Your adrenaline rises, your face flushes, and your voice grows taut, all because of a memory of some past transgression. Yet in the present moment, there has been no offense or misdeed. Disregard the past and you'll see that your Personal Priorities await. Don't they deserve your attention more than some incident from a bygone day?

While it's difficult to forgive the past, it can be even harder to trust the future. My telling you not to worry is like telling the rain to stop falling. But where do your worries take you? To a future you can't foretell. And even though none of us can predict tomorrow, sometimes we presume that the worst will happen. We create a fear and then live it, when in truth, nothing bad has happened. A wonderful observation about worry has been attributed to both Winston Churchill and Mark Twain. One of these wise men commented, "I have had many troubles in my life, and some of them have actually happened." Inevitably, you will bear your share of troubles in your life. Why let worry create even more?

Banning worry is much easier said than done. The week I was writing this chapter I was on call for jury duty. At 5 o'clock one evening, I was notified I had to be at the county courthouse at 8 the next morning. I freaked out. I had been hoping to bypass the obligation entirely. I'd even visualized invisibility so I wouldn't be one of the citizens they called. After I got the summons, I pictured myself sitting in the waiting area of some courtroom for the next three days, unable to accomplish anything. My family and I were moving in three weeks. I had no time to fulfill my civic responsibilities. How could the universe have let me down? I spent the entire evening stressed out and short tempered with my family. All night I tossed and turned, plagued by worry. The next day, I reported to jury duty, was never called, and was released by early afternoon. I had wasted more time worrying about the event than the so-called ordeal had lasted. My family, my Personal Priorities, and I all had suffered needlessly.

So the next time you catch yourself fretting about the immutable past or an uncertain future event, observe how those emotions are robbing you of the present. Ask yourself, "Is this how I want to spend my precious time?" Surely you have some Personal Priority that you would rather embrace.

Keep Asking, "Am I Making the Choices I Want?"

I don't want to get to the end of my life and find that I lived just the length of it. I want to have lived the width of it as well.
Diane Ackerman

Ultimately, how you choose to spend your time is how you choose to live your life. Creating balance is a constant challenge, not because it's essentially difficult, but because you receive so little support from the outside world. That is why you have to work so hard to encourage yourself. Having balance is striving to meet your own expectations and no one else's. It is recognizing that when others disapprove or disagree with your choices, it's probably because they don't know or respect the value of your Personal Priorities.

Once you become conscious of how you spend your time, you realize you are constantly making choices. This realization is the power you need to maintain balance in your life. As you walk away from your workplace in order to go to your piano lessons, you are choosing what trade-offs you make. As you leave the day-care center hearing your toddler whine, "Mommy, don't go," you are following the path you picked. As you apply for a new job, or decide not to apply for a new job, you are selecting the way you want to live. Recognizing these choices, appreciating the power in these choices is wonderful. You realize that the essence of your life is yours to cherish and protect. And you will do a better job of this than anyone else in the world.

But how do you know you are making the right choices? Sometimes your inner voice speaks with great clarity and you have no doubts. Other times, however, your internal voice may itself be divided, torn by a longing for conflicting goals. In these cases, my advice is to step away from your current dilemma and ask yourself, "What will really matter to me in five years? Or ten? Or even more?" By granting yourself a longer perspective, you will see a broader pattern. And within that pattern, your answer might become very clear.

One way to prompt yourself to take a longer perspective is to imagine you are 80 years old. As an 80-year-old, what is your opinion of the choices you're making now? Are you devoting your time to the most important aspects of life, those that will create joy for you over the next decades? Or are you spending your hours on less critical matters that may loom large today but will wither in significance with the passing years?

Listening to Your Inner Voice of Wisdom

Each person carries his own doctor within.
Albert Schweitzer

In my Balanced Life workshops, I ask the participants to write a letter to themselves from the perspective they would have when they're 80 years old. (At the end of this chapter, I'll ask you to do the same.) Frequently people are surprised by the emotions this exercise evokes. There is something about stepping away from our daily existence that makes us appreciate how precious our life truly is. At some point, we've all longed for advice from a wise mentor who loves us intensely and understands us completely. This exercise proves that the wisdom and love we long for is already inside us. We only have to let the voice come out.

Some of the people who attended my Balanced Life classes shared their letters with me. As you listen to the insight and tenderness of their words, think of what you might want to say to yourself.

Dear Young Nicole,
    You have worried so much about what you felt you had to accomplish. You had to have a certain job, lifestyle, and marriage by age 30. So your life didn't happen as you planned. So what! You are still young!
    Realize that you have so much life ahead of you. Stop living by others' expectations whether it is society, parents, or your friends. Stop worrying so much. Laugh more and accept that it's okay to cry sometimes. Life passes by too

*quickly. Why not spend the valuable time on your own
happiness rather than worrying about everyone else's?*

*You have heard before, "Lord, grant me the strength to
change the things I can and accept the things I cannot."
Realize that you can change things more than you think. It's
okay to spend time on yourself. Take a nap. Call a friend.
Travel. Empower yourself to make the changes to your life.
No one else is responsible for you. No prince in shining
armor is going to make everything better. Only you can.*

(signed)
Old Nicole

In her letter, this young, newly pregnant woman does an
admirable job in counseling herself:

My dearest,

*You are at a crossroads in your life right now. Starting a
family is a wonderful thing. Now it is especially important to
stay true to your values and what you believe in while you
try to balance a baby, work, and school. Don't take on
more than you can. Don't let perfectionism cloud things.*

*Be kind to yourself over the next six months—there will
be times when you will feel that you don't know what you're
doing, that you can't handle parenthood, when you'll have
periods of guilt for not being at work and identity confusion
over this new role as "mother." Consider one of your
Personal Priorities as "Continuing to learn new things," and
it will help you through.*

Signed with love

Here is another piece of wisdom written by a man who
sounds almost surprised that he knows so much:

Hi Dan,

Slow down, relax, and listen. I want to give you some advice for how you handle yourself over the next forty-five years. You need to simplify your life. You need to stop thinking about how quickly you can get things done because it's never done!

- You think: If I get promoted, I'll be happy and successful. Wrong! A promotion does not equal happiness.
- You think: If I could only get this house done, I'll be happy. Wrong! Building your home as you go will make you happy. It will never be done.
- You think: If I could get my savings to $500,000, I could quit and retire. Wrong! Money does not equal retirement and retirement does not equal happiness.

You have to live life as you go. Stop looking for the "end of the line." The only end will be when you pass. Don't fall into being pessimistic. Enjoy each moment, each day. If you don't, you will look back with regrets. You'll have missed living.

From Dan

Giving yourself permission to look at your life through a longer lens creates many insights. These insights will lead you to wiser choices. You will recognize what is truly important to you and make the decisions that help you become who you want to be. You will spot the ironies that toy with you daily. Perspective also allows you to forgive others and yourself. You realize that many of the wrongdoings that seem immense today will shrink to nothingness in the vista of time.

Making the choices you want, being conscious of how you spend your time, and being mindful of your Personal Priorities are what you must do to create balance in your life. That and the courage and stamina to stick with your convictions. For if you don't stand up for yourself, who will?

The Secret to Living a Balanced Life

We have our brush and colors, paint paradise, and in we go.
Nikos Kazantzakis

I've started each chapter of this book with a parable that serves as a metaphor for the lesson I want you to understand. I will end our time with one last story.

HOLDING A LIFE IN YOUR HANDS

Many, many years ago in a small village, some soldiers are harassing a rabbi. One of the soldiers catches a young bird and clasps it in his hands so that it's entirely hidden from view.

"Rabbi," he teases, "since you are supposed to be so smart, tell us about the bird I am holding. Is it alive or is it dead?"

The rabbi ponders the question. He knows if he says the bird is dead, the soldier will let it fly away. On the other hand, if he says it is alive, the soldier will crush and kill it. Finally, he has his answer.

"I will tell you," the rabbi responds, "whether the bird is alive or dead. The answer is in your hands."

Will you find the balance you need in your life?
The answer is in your hands.

May you live a life you love, today and every day.

Exploration Exercise

All of the exercises for this chapter are designed to help you maintain balance in your life, even as you finish reading the book.

Looking in the Mirror

This is a meditation and writing exercise. For this one, you will need a pen or pencil, paper, and a mailing envelope. You will be imagining that you are 80 years old. Then as that 80-year-old person, you are writing a letter of advice to the younger you, the you of today. The advice is about the importance of having balance in your life.

Try to get someone to read the meditation to you, or tape it and replay it for yourself, or read it to yourself, pausing and visualizing the scene between the paragraphs. Or listen to a similar meditation on the Web site: www.comingupforair.com. After the meditation, you can start writing.

Now starting writing the letter to yourself from the you who is 80 years old. When you are done, put it in the envelope and address it to yourself.

The next step is to forget about this letter until a month or two goes by. Then you can reread it as a reminder of your search for a balanced life. There are a couple of ways to make this happen. One is to give it to someone you trust and ask him or her to mail it to you in a month. Another idea is to put it somewhere that you only access about once a month, say your bill-paying file or with some occasionally used sporting equipment. A third option is to put a future date on the envelope as a reminder of when to open it and put it in your desk drawer. Even if it is misplaced for a few months it will still have the desired effect on you when you reread it.

IMAGINE YOU ARE 80

Sit comfortably in your chair. Put both feet on the ground, arms at your sides or resting on your lap. Take a deep breath. Let it out. Take another deep breath, deep into your abdomen, then to the bottom of your lungs. Slowly fill your lungs. Now even more slowly, let it out. Take another breath just like that one.

I want you to let your mind travel into the future. Much time has passed between now and then. Your working days are in the past, nothing but memories now. Different presidents have come and gone. You have seen many, many years go by. You are 80 years old.

Imagine what you are like when you are 80. You are still healthy, still alert, but wiser, much wiser. You have seen the many sides of life. You have gone through wonderful periods, and frankly, some periods that were just hard. But they are behind you now. You are enjoying the present, wherever you might be. You are involved in your life. You greet every morning with joy, the beginning of a new day.

Now, as an 80-year-old, you are looking back on your life, recollecting some of your memories. You remember the time when you were struggling to have balance in your life. You smile gently at the memory—seeing yourself as a younger person, striving to do what was best for you, trying to learn to understand yourself and how you related to your home and work lives.

Now imagine, as an 80-year-old, what advice could you now give the younger you? What would you tell yourself about what is really important? Not what seemed important then, but what really counts, now that you have the wise perspective of an 80-year-old. What advice would you give about your career, your home life, your health, and where you find joy?

As you think about this advice, remember it is coming from your self, someone who knows and loves you better than anyone else in the world. So what would you say?

After you have thought about this for a while, take two or three deep breaths and when you are ready, open your eyes.

Commute Questions

Go back over the various Commute Questions from the prior chapters. Glean out the ones that still interest you and copy them onto index cards. Then put them somewhere so that they will accompany you on your commute, in your purse, briefcase, or glove compartment. Then if you find yourself struggling with a particular balance question, they are there waiting for you to cue your inner resources for the answer.

Action Step

If you haven't done so already, schedule some dates, appointments, or classes that allow you to focus on your Personal Priorities. Have them extend over several weeks or months. Maintain your commitment to keep those dates, and keep some balance in your life.

> To me, having a balanced life means feeling at peace with myself every day of my life.
>
> A 40-year-old single woman who treasures both her friendships and her job

Suggested Reading

I'm an avid reader of self-help books and have probably gone through a hundred or more over the last ten years. If the author provides even one idea that I incorporate into my life permanently, I consider the book well worth my time.

The following books are among the best I have read and provided me with lots of guidance in improving my life. I have lent or given copies of all of these to many friends and colleagues. I hope you find them helpful as well.

TO MAKE THE MOST OF YOUR WORK

Covey, Steven. *Seven Habits of Highly Effective People*. Simon & Schuster, 1989. A great book that provides a very effective approach to life and time management.

Heider, John. *The Tao of Leadership—Lao Tzu's Tao Te Ching Adopted for a New Age*. Humanics Publishing Group, 1986. Ancient teachings adapted to apply to the modern workplace.

Ray, Michael, and Myers, Rochelle. *Creativity in Business*. Doubleday, 1989. An excellent guide that helps you be a more creative problem solver and a more centered individual.

TO MAKE THE MOST OF EACH DAY

Breathnach, Sarah Ban. *Simple Abundance: A Daybook of Comfort and Joy.* Warner Books, 1995. Targeted, but not limited, to women, this book takes the reader day by day through a journey to discover his/her authentic self.

Carlson, Richard. *Don't Sweat the Small Stuff . . . and It's All Small Stuff: Simple Ways to Keep the Little Things from Taking Over Your Life.* Hyperion, 1997. A great set of practices that help you understand what really matters. Adopting even ten out of the hundred suggestions will change your approach to life.

St. James, Elaine. *Simplify Your Life—100 Ways to Slow Down and Enjoy the Things That Really Matter.* Hyperion, 1994. You are bound to discover at least a few ideas in this book that will make your life simpler and save you time.

TO ENRICH YOUR HOME

Culp, Stephanie. *How to Get Organized When You Don't Have the Time.* Writer's Digest Books, 1986. Practical suggestions on how to make your life more organized and efficient. An easy read.

Robinson, Jo, and Staeheli, Jean Coppock (Contributor). *Unplug the Christmas Machine.* Quill, 1991. An outstanding book that takes much of the stress away from the Christmas holidays.

Scott, Anne. *Serving Fire: Food for Thought, Body, and Soul.* Celestial Arts, 1994. Offers suggestions on how to recenter yourself around the home and hearth.

FOR JOB AND/OR LIFE CHANGES

Boldt, Laurence G. *How to Find the Work You Love.* Arkana/Penguin Books, 1996. Inspiring words on how to find the job that helps fulfill your purpose in life. By the author of *Zen and the Art of Making a Living.*

Bolles, Richard Nelson. *What Color Is Your Parachute?* Ten Speed Press, 1998. Perennial best-seller for job seekers.

Bolles, Richard Nelson. *How to Find Your Mission in Life*. Ten Speed Press, 1992. This 55-page book helps you get a better understanding of what it means to have a mission in your life, whether or not you're thinking of changing jobs (an appendix from *What Color Is Your Parachute?*).

Sher, Barbara, and Gottlieb, Annie. *Wishcraft: How to Get What You Really Want*. Ballantine Books, 1986. A very intriguing approach on how to design what you want from life, then gearing yourself up to go get it.

Index